THE ART AND SCIENCE OF

TEMPURA

A COMPREHENSIVE GUIDE TO
INGREDIENTS, TECHNIQUES AND EQUIPMENT

Technical Director Takashi Nakagawa
Text Hidemi Sato and Mitose Tsuchida

TUTTLE Publishing
Tokyo | Rutland, Vermont | Singapore

Contents

CHAPTER 4

THE BATTER

CHAPTER 5

THE FRYING OIL

CHAPTER 6

DEEP-FRYING TECHNIQUES

CHAPTER 7

KAKIAGE MIXED FRITTERS

NOTES

- This book is based on the methods of Chef Takashi Nakagawa of the restaurant Tempura Nakagawa, but there are many different techniques and interpretations when it comes to tempura.
- The focus is on the Edomae style of thoroughly frying ingredients in sesame oil.
- In some cases, the explanations prioritize terminology used by professional chefs.
- The sentence below each chapter title features a quote from Chef Nakagawa that reflects the theme.
- Data on ingredient size and temperature reflect measurements taken on the day of testing and may vary depending on conditions and environment.
- The sizes of vegetables are not specified.

INTRODUCTION

THE HISTORY OF TEMPURA

"We inherit traditions from those who came before—
and pass them on to those who come next."

—Chef Takashi Nakagawa

The History of Tempura

It is said that tempura first became an accessible food for ordinary people with the appearance of yatai street-food stalls in the Edo period (1603–1868). Whether as a home-cooked side dish or a delicacy showcasing a chef's skill at a restaurant, tempura — now known around the world — has a deep and fascinating history.

The origins of tempura

Before discussing the history of tempura, let's start with this question: since when has deep-fried food existed in Japan? Oil is a necessity when it comes to deep-frying, but the Shosoin treasure house (the repository of Todai-ji Temple in Nara), holds documentary evidence of oil being used for cooking (rather than lighting lamps) as far back as the Nara and early Heian periods, around the eighth to ninth centuries. Also around that time, fried sweets as snacks were introduced from Tang Dynasty China, and it is likely that these were deep-fried.

In the Kamakura period (1185–1333), *shojin ryori* or Zen Buddhist vegetarian cuisine was introduced to Japan, consisting of vegetable and tofu dishes cooked with sesame oil. At the time, the ingredients would have been fried "uncoated," without any batter or breading.

It wasn't until the sixteenth century that battered tempura-like food first appeared. From the late Muromachi period (1333–1573) to the Azuchi-Momoyama period (1573–1584), Portuguese and Spanish trading ships began to arrive in Japan. The southern Europeans introduced a style of dish in which fish and vegetables were coated with a flour-based batter and deep-fried in oil. This method of cooking was first introduced in the port city of Nagasaki, on Japan's southernmost main island of Kyushu, and came to be called "Nagasaki Tempura." It is considered to be the prototype of Japanese tempura. This kind of tempura was made with a batter that was quite different from the type of batter used today. It was made of flour, eggs, sugar, sake and salt.

There are several theories about the origins of the word *tempura*. One is that it is a corruption of the Portuguese word *tempero*, meaning "cooking" or "seasoning," which is consistent with the way the batter for Nagasaki-style tempura is seasoned before it is fried. However, there is no definitive documentary evidence for this etymology.

In those days, oil was an extremely precious commodity in Japan. Therefore tempura, which requires a large amount of oil, was a luxury food, one which was rarely available to ordinary people. It would take a little time before tempura eventually spread to the Osaka region and then onward to Tokyo.

The increasing popularity of tempura

It wasn't until the mid-Edo period (1603–1868), when oil production increased, that tempura became more widely available in Japan. As sesame oil and rapeseed oil came to be produced in large quantities, the production of tempura increased.

Buto is a Chinese snack that came over to Japan in the eighth century. It is made with rice flour, shaped like a gyoza dumpling, and deep-fried in sesame oil. It is still a well-known traditional confection today, and is sometimes used as a sacred offering to the gods.

The rapeseed plant was originally grown as a vegetable, but during the Edo period, as the method for extracting oil from the seeds was developed, it came to be commonly grown as an oil-producing plant.

Food stalls were developing around the same period too. In the Edo period, many people lived in small, narrow tenement houses called *nagaya* where kitchens were almost nonexistent, or very basic, so only simple meals could be prepared. Nagaya were made of wood, so cooking with fire was frowned upon. That's why food stalls selling items like tempura or *kabayaki* grilled eel—which required fire—were highly valued. Having food cooked at a food stall rather than at home also meant there was no problem with smoke and no need to worry about disposing of used cooking oil. Besides tempura and kabayaki, sushi and soba noodles were popular food-stall items too, and you can see the origins of modern specialty restaurants in these food stalls.

At the time, tempura sold at food stalls had a thick, heavy batter, similar to the coating used for Nagasaki-style tempura. Since the batter was made by kneading flour and water together, the gluten made it sticky and caused a thick layer to form—one can imagine it being quite dense. In fact, if you look at ukiyo-e prints depicting the period, you'll see skewered pieces with this "heavy-style" batter. These were eaten dipped in *tentsuyu* tempura sauce.

The tempura ingredients used in Edo (the former name for Tokyo) came from a variety of seafood caught in Edo Bay—in other words, from Edomae (literally, "in front of Edo"). This seafood included tiger shrimp, gizzard shad, Japanese whiting and sea eel. Over time, the thick, doughy batter became thinner and thinner. The people of Edo developed a preference for tempura with a crispy texture, fried in rich-tasting sesame oil. This has led to the current use of sesame oil for the style of tempura that has become common to the Tokyo area, which is still referred to as "Edomae tempura" today.

On the other hand, in the Kansai region (the Osaka–Kyoto area) people have traditionally preferred their tempura cooked with light-tasting soy bean or cottonseed oil, and merely sprinkled with salt.

In fact, it is said that the tempura we know today that is dipped in a batter made by mixing flour with liquid originates from roadside sellers in the Kansai region. However, this was differentiated from tempura and called *tsuke-age*. So what was tempura in the Kansai region? According to the book *Morisada manko* (Morisada's

Sketches) written at the end of the Edo period by Morisada Kitagawa: "The tempura of the Kansai region refers to fish-paste cakes that are deep-fried without any coating, or what are called in Edo *satsuma-age*."

This remains a confusing matter even today: what is called satsuma-age in the Tokyo region is called tempura in the Osaka region and in Japan's southernmost main island of Kyushu.

Kinpura, a high-end tempura

By the mid–Edo period, tempura had become so popular that street vendors began to open their own restaurants. The consumer base for the dish had spread to people from all walks of life, from the working classes to high-ranking samurai.

To reflect this trend, a luxurious version of tempura called *kinpura* (literally, "gold tempura") was invented. Buckwheat (soba) flour was used

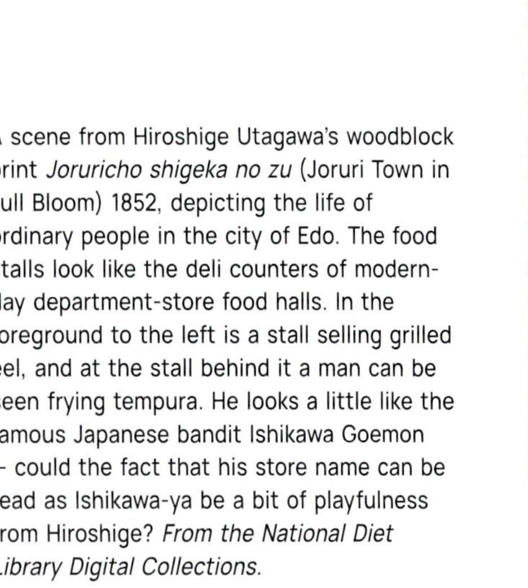

A scene from Hiroshige Utagawa's woodblock print *Joruricho shigeka no zu* (Joruri Town in Full Bloom) 1852, depicting the life of ordinary people in the city of Edo. The food stalls look like the deli counters of modern-day department-store food halls. In the foreground to the left is a stall selling grilled eel, and at the stall behind it a man can be seen frying tempura. He looks a little like the famous Japanese bandit Ishikawa Goemon – could the fact that his store name can be read as Ishikawa-ya be a bit of playfulness from Hiroshige? *From the National Diet Library Digital Collections.*

instead of wheat flour, and the yolks of eggs— a luxury food at the time—were added to make the batter for frying. In 1853, a book that ranked various eating places in Edo titled *Edo ryuko saizenki* (Selected Trends of Edo) lists a store called Kinpura Goma, which also mentions prices: "Various pricing to suit all budgets, from 100 to 56 *mon* per person."

The sum of 100 mon was the equivalent of about 2,000 yen in today's money, so compared to stalls where one tempura item could be bought for 4 mon (about 80 yen), you can see that Kinpura Goma's prices were quite expensive.

Interestingly, the name *kinpura* gained favor, and over time came to refer not only to tempura made with buckwheat flour and egg yolk, but also to versions using potato starch, only egg yolk, or camellia oil—anything that resulted in an overall golden color. There was even *ginpura* (silver tempura), made with egg whites.

The high-end trend continued through the nineteenth century, and the number of new tempura restaurants continued to grow. Tempura started to be offered in traditional *ryotei* restaurants, and in small *kappo* restaurants with stylish premises. Tokyo's most famous tempura restaurants included Hashizen in Shinbashi, founded in 1832 and closed in 2002; and Tenkin in Ginza, established in 1864 and closed in 1970.

A tempura shop, showing thickly battered skewers of tempura is depicted in the painting *Shokunin tsukushi ekotoba* (Chronicle of Artisans) by Kuwagata Keisai and others, early 1800s. *From the National Diet Library Digital Collections.*

Tempura up to the present day

Tempura continued to be popular in the Meiji period (1868–1912). The Tokyo tempura restaurants Nakasei in Asakusa and Tenkuni in Ginza, were established in 1870 and 1885 respectively, and both of these establishments are still in operation today.

Following the Great Kanto Earthquake of 1923, the style of tempura began to change. Food stalls started to disappear, while the number of tempura restaurants increased. They were especially prevalent in and around Tokyo's Ginza district; including Ginza Tenichi, which opened in 1930 and is still in existence today. Many restaurants from the Osaka region also expanded into Tokyo, bringing with them the Osaka style of tempura: lightly fried in a mild oil (not sesame oil), and served with salt instead of tentsuyu dipping sauce. Around this time, vegetable tempura—using ingredients such as ginkgo nuts—also started to appear. Though some shops in Tokyo had served fried vegetables before this, it hadn't been common. The style of lightly fried tempura served with salt became widely popular. However, the perception that Edomae tempura is made with sesame oil has persisted, and even today, restaurants that maintain the tradition of Tokyo tempura insist on the use of sesame oil.

By the way, there is a high-end style of tempura called *ozashiki* tempura—the word *ozashiki* refers to a gathering held in a private tatami-matted room. It is said that this style started around 1860, when chefs would take ingredients and utensils directly to their customers' residences to serve them freshly fried tempura right there.

A frying station would be set up on a table in a tatami room and surrounded by a semicircular counter. The floor under the table was sunken so the guests could dangle their feet down and sit comfortably. This setup was essentially the same as modern counter-style tempura where the chef fries the food right in front of the customers, who can enjoy it piping hot and freshly made. The chef and diners were face to face as though they were at a food stall—but with the added comfort of a seated setting. This arrangement served as a kind of cultural salon for many intellectuals and artists, both from Japan and abroad. Watching the batter-coated ingredients sizzle right in front of you in hot oil made tempura not just a meal, but also a form of entertainment.

The ozashiki style of serving tempura took root from the end of the nineteenth century, leading to today's counter-centered Edomae (or Tokyo-style) tempura.

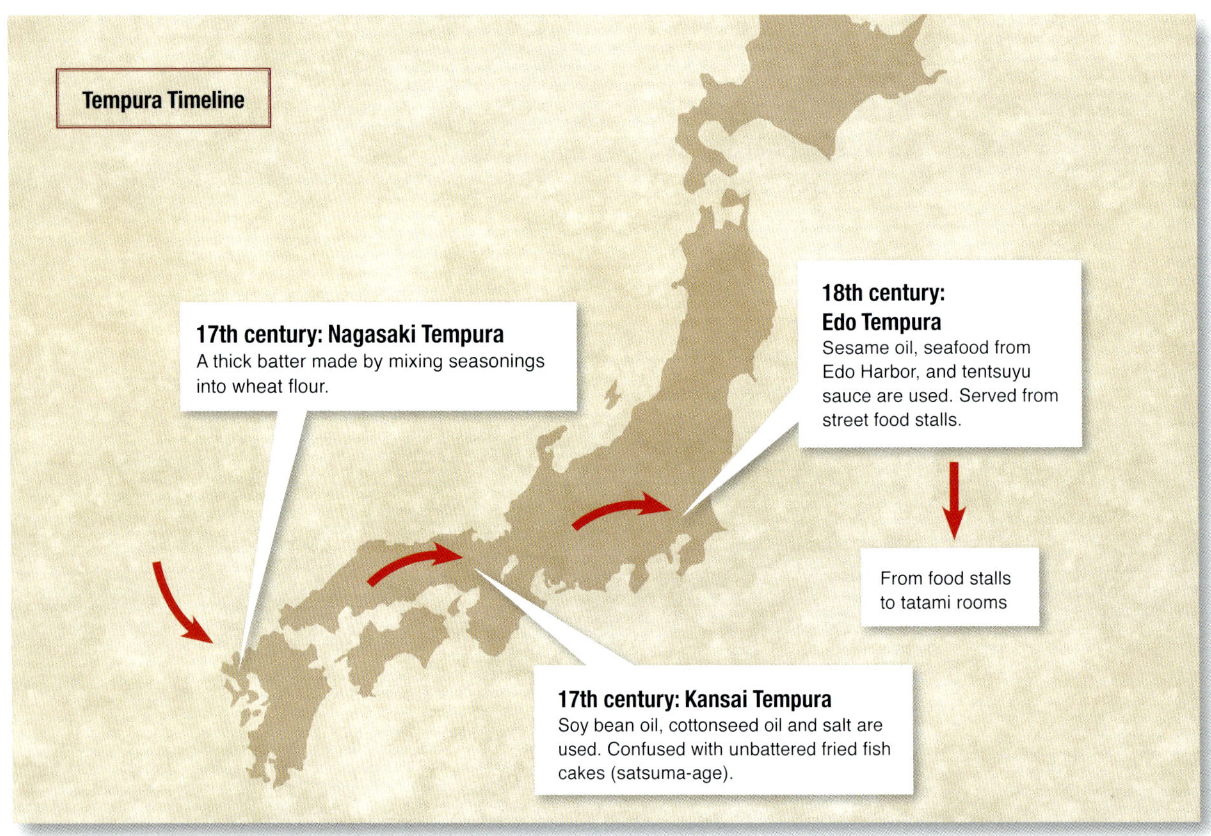

At the tatami-room counter of the famous Ginza Tenichi restaurant in 1953. From front to back: writer Ton Satomi, British potter Bernard Leach, novelist and playwright Saneatsu Mushanokoji, potter Shoji Hamada, and philosopher Tetsuzo Tanigawa. Tempura restaurants with tatami-room counters were like salons for intellectuals.
Photo credit: Ginza Tenichi

The food stalls that were the origin of such counter service continued to exist even after World War II, especially during the black market boom in the immediate postwar period. However, at the time of the 1964 Tokyo Olympics, street stalls were cleared out en masse, and most tempura stalls disappeared along with them.

The global popularity of tempura

In the early twentieth century in Japan, housewives also began to make tempura at home. Recipes for tempura made with ingredients such as sardines, shrimp, tomato and more are included in the 1931 cookbook *Katei ryori senshoku* (Home Cooking: A Thousand Dishes), published by Shufunotomo-sha, Ltd.

By around 1960, a Japanese food boom had begun in the United States. From that time onward, tempura has become widely known around the world. While tempura had traditionally focused on seafood, more and more vegetables—once considered part of a separate category known as *shojin-age* (Buddhist-style vegetable tempura)—began to be used as well. Nowadays, tempura specialty restaurants are even featured in the Michelin Guide Tokyo.

With a greater variety of flours and oils now available, and with an ever-expanding range of ingredients, we are constantly seeing creative and innovative tempura crafted by skilled chefs.

After a long history, Japanese tempura has become beloved worldwide—ranging from a simple homemade side dish to a refined specialty served in high-end restaurants.

CHAPTER 1

TEMPURA INGREDIENTS

"Working with simple, top quality ingredients is a joy."

—Chef Takashi Nakagawa

魚介類

Seafood

The natural flavors of seasonal seafood are sealed in by tempura's unique method of cooking in high-temperature oil. Page numbers are given for preparation and cooking methods.

穴子
Conger Eel (*anago*)
pages 46 and 134

白魚
Japanese Icefish (*shirauo*)
page 140

鱚
Japanese Whiting (*kisu*)
pages 42 and 128

車海老
Tiger Shrimp (*kuruma ebi*)
page 120

芝海老
Small White
Shrimp (*shiba ebi*)
page 210

目鯒
Big-eyed Flathead (*megochi*)
pages 50 and 156

貝柱
Scallops (*kaibashira*)
page 206

鮑
Abalone (*awabi*)
pages 66 and 162

沙魚
Yellowfin Goby (*haze*)
pages 68 and 152

稚鮎
Young Sweetfish (*chiayu*)
page 146

障泥烏賊
Bigfin Reef Squid (*aori-ika*)
pages 58 and 132

岩牡蠣
Japanese Rock Oysters (*iwagaki*)
page 148

墨烏賊
Golden Cuttlefish (*sumi-ika*)
pages 54 and 130

銀宝
Tidepool Gunnel (*ginpo*)
pages 70 and 154

鱧
Pike Conger (*hamo*)
page 150
河豚
Puffer Fish Milt (*fugu shirako*)
page 144
白子
Milt (*shirako*)
鱈
Cod Milt (*tara shirako*)
page 142

雲丹
Sea Urchin (*uni*)
page 158

How to Prepare Cod Milt

Rinsing cod milt in soy sauce helps to remove the sliminess, and also helps gets rid of any fishy odor.

How to Open Oysters

1 Place the oyster on a flat surface. Insert an oyster knife or a table knife into the gap between the upper and lower shells.

2 Move the knife back and forth slowly along the inside of the upper shell. Cut the adductor muscle in the center to detach the oyster meat from the shell, then remove the upper shell.

3 As for step 2, insert the knife along the inside of the bottom shell. Cut the adductor muscle and carefully detach the oyster meat.

野菜類

Vegetables

Tempura made with vegetables, known as *shojin-age* (Zen Buddhist-style vegan fried food) is distinct from Edomae (Edo or Tokyo style) tempura, but the unique flavors, aromas and colors of the vegetables featured here make them ideal for this style of cooking. Page numbers are given for preparation and cooking methods.

薩摩芋
Japanese Sweet Potato
(*satsumaimo*)
page 170

南瓜
Kabocha Squash (*kabocha*)
page 174

モロッコ隠元
Flat Green Beans
(*morokko ingen*)
page 178

茄子
Eggplant (*nasu*)
page 180

万願寺唐辛子
Manganji Pepper
(*Manganji togarashi*)
page 168
蓮根
Lotus Root (*renkon*)
page 184
ペコロス
Pearl Onion
(*pekorosu*)
page 182
アスパラガス
Asparagus (*asuparagasu*)
page 176

谷中生姜
Young Ginger
(*yanaka shoga*)
page 186

大葉
Green Shiso Leaf (*oba*)
page 158

銀杏
Ginkgo Nuts (*ginnan*)
pages 72 and 166

松茸
Matsutake Mushrooms
(*matsutake*)
page 196

茸
Mushrooms
(*kinoko*)

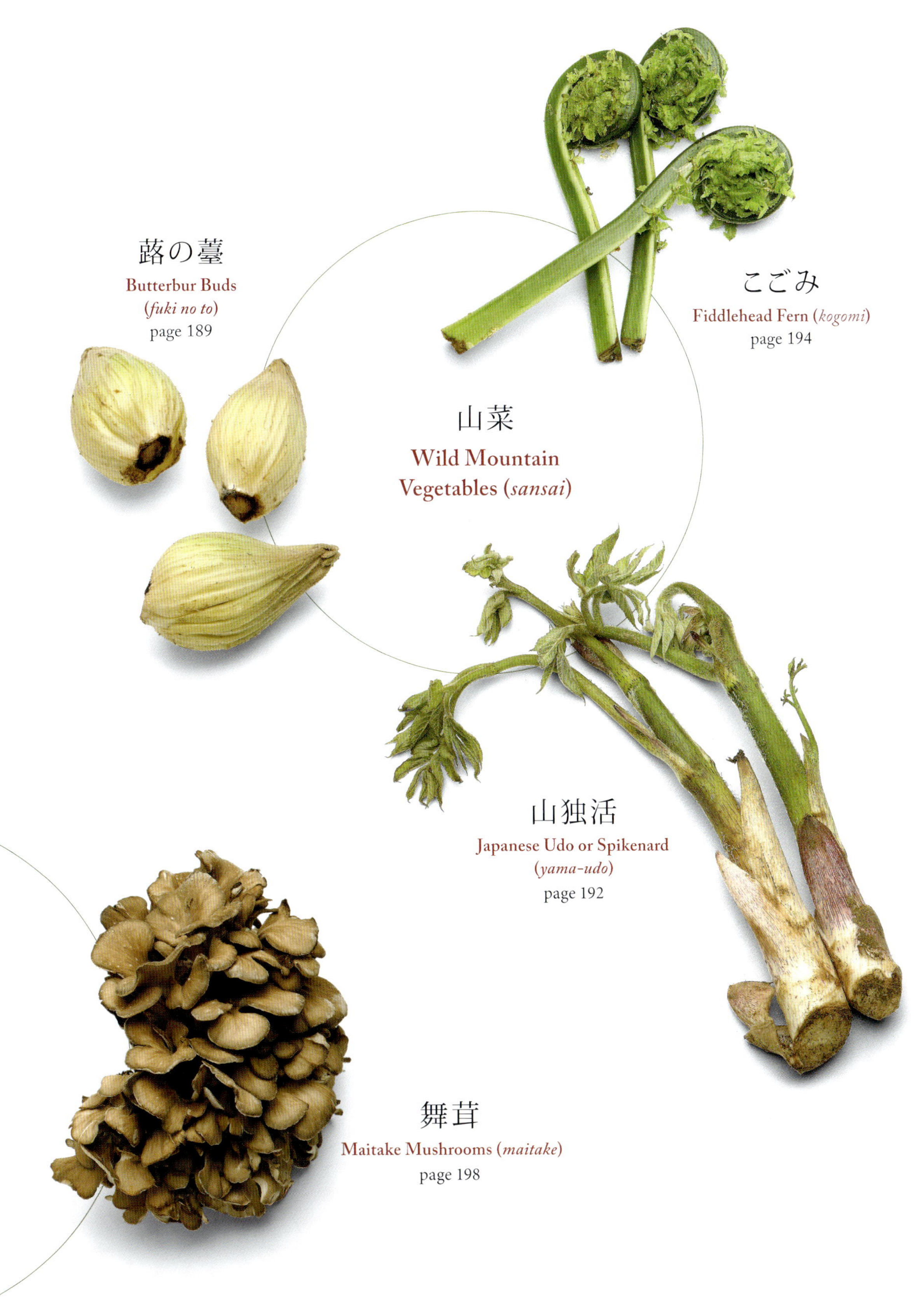
蕗の薹
Butterbur Buds
(*fuki no to*)
page 189
こごみ
Fiddlehead Fern (*kogomi*)
page 194
山菜
Wild Mountain
Vegetables (*sansai*)
山独活
Japanese Udo or Spikenard
(*yama-udo*)
page 192
舞茸
Maitake Mushrooms (*maitake*)
page 198

What Is Edomae Tempura?

The term *Edomae*, used for tempura, sushi, and kabayaki grilled eel, has various interpretations. Originally, it referred to the waters in front of the city of Edo (the old name for Tokyo), but both the geography and the fishing grounds have changed since then. So what does Edomae really mean?

The word *Edomae* originally meant the sea in front of Edo Castle, the symbolic heart of the city of Edo. A document from the fish market at Nihonbashi addressed to government authorities during the Edo period (1603–1868) states, "From Shinagawa promontory in the west and Fukagawa promontory in the east—this area in between we call Edomae."

Edo was a city of waterways, with around sixty rivers including major ones like the Tama, Sumida, Nakagawa, Edogawa and Arakawa. These rivers carried sediment and nutrients, forming vast tidal flats, rich habitats where fish would gather. Fishermen targeted these waters and brought in their catch to the Nihonbashi riverbank district and other riverbanks located in various parts of Edo. It was this bounty that nurtured the development of Edo's tempura and sushi cultures.

Today, however, the area in front of the site of the old Edo Castle—where the Imperial Palace is now located—has been almost completely reclaimed by landfill. And with advancements in fishing vessels, fishing grounds have moved farther offshore. So the historical definition of Edomae no longer applies in a strict sense—its meaning has shifted to suit modern times.

In 1953, Tokyo's Tsukiji fish market organized a meeting with fish traders and brokers from fishing ports along the Tokyo Bay coast to establish a new definition for Edomae. They agreed that the area of sea within a line connecting Kannonzaki Lighthouse in Kanagawa Prefecture and the summit of Mount Nokogiri in Chiba Prefecture would be designated as Edomae waters.

Tokyo Bay can be divided into two main areas, one of which is the inner bay along the line between Cape Futtsu in Chiba Prefecture and Kannonzaki in Kanagawa Prefecture. This inner bay is shallow, and thought to closely resemble the marine environment of the original Edomae area. That said, at present, the term "Tokyo Bay" is most appropriately used to refer to the entire area stretching from the inner bay outward to the line connecting Cape Tsurugisaki in Kanagawa and Cape Sunosaki in Chiba.

In 2004, the Ministry of Agriculture, Forestry and Fisheries established the "Tokyo Bay Restoration Review Committee—Food Culture Subcommittee," where the meaning of Edomae was once again discussed. It was ultimately agreed that Edomae refers to all of Tokyo Bay, and that all seafood caught within this bay should be considered Edomae fish.

Tokyo Bay, enclosed by the Miura and Boso Peninsulas, is relatively sheltered compared to the open Pacific Ocean. It is less affected by strong waves and tides, making it a calm and stable environment that helps produce seafood with tender, delicate flesh—a quality that underpins the flavor and appeal of Edomae cuisine.

Main Fishing Methods and Fish Species of the Current Edomae Area

Purse seine or round haul net	Japanese sardine, Japanese anchovy, gizzard shad, horse mackerel
Encircling gillnet	Flathead mullet, halfbeak, Japanese sea bass
Bottom trawling	Flathead, white croaker, beltfish, marbled flounder, stone flounder
Eel trap	Conger eel
Line fishing	Rockfish, black rockfish, greenling, Japanese whiting, surfperch, thread-sail filefish, yellowfin goby

Seasonal Calendar for Tempura Ingredients

Tempura ingredients have been carefully selected over time to suit this cooking style. Ingredients are chosen to capture the peak seasonal flavors from Japan's seas and mountains, sealed in a crisp coating and quickly fried to perfection. This is the true appeal of tempura. Seasonality varies depending on the region of origin, the weather and the year.

Ingredient \ Month	January	February	March	April
Tiger Shrimp				
Japanese Whiting				
Conger Eel				
Big-eyed Flathead				
Sea Urchin				
Abalone				
Japanese Rock Oyster				
Tidepool Gunnel				
Japanese Icefish				
Cod Milt				
Puffer Fish Milt				
Golden Cuttlefish				
Bigfin Reef Squid				
Young Sweetfish				
Yellowfin Goby				
Pike Conger				
Scallop				
Small White Shrimp				
Wild Mountain Vegetables				
Matsutake Mushrooms				

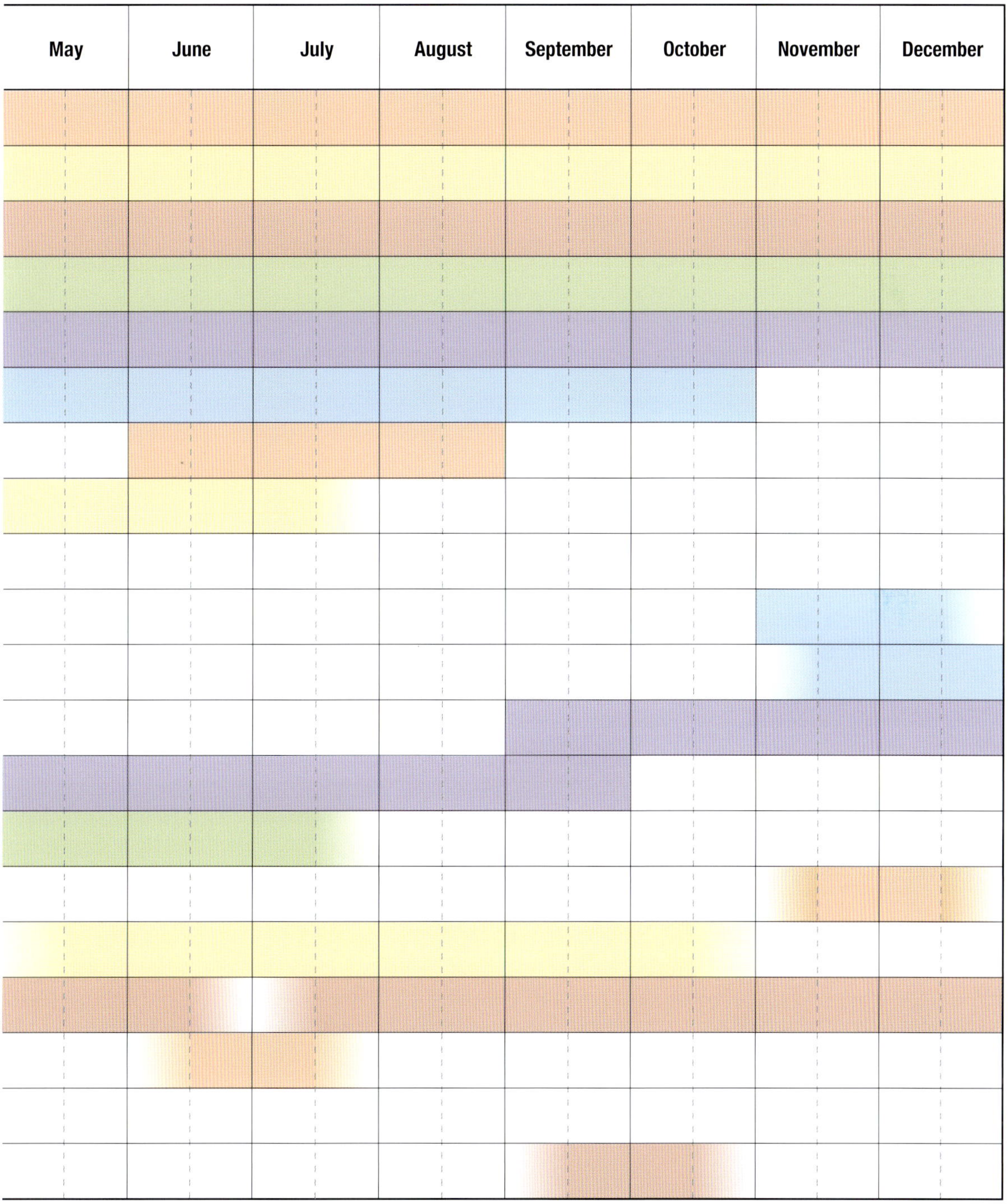

May	June	July	August	September	October	November	December

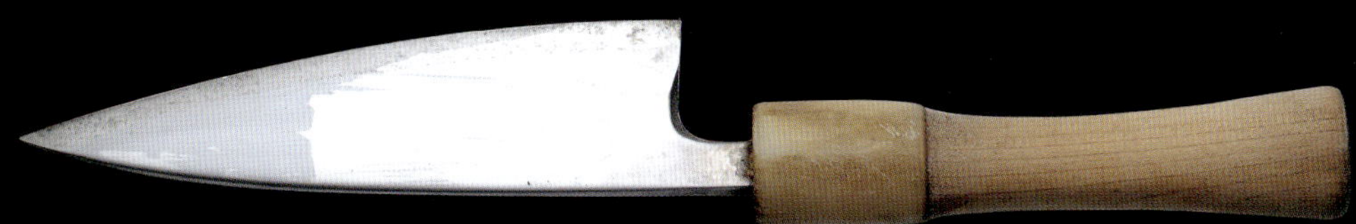

CHAPTER 2

TEMPURA KITCHEN TOOLS

"The tools you use should feel like an extension of your hand."

—Chef Takashi Nakagawa

Pot (*nabe*)

The Pot

For tempura, it's essential to use a pot that doesn't drop in temperature too quickly, even when cold ingredients are added one after another. The pot should allow the heat to be kept relatively stable.

Pots are chosen based on materials and thicknesses that efficiently transfer heat to the tempura ingredients, along with shapes and depths designed for smooth, effective frying.

Two types of heat sources are widely used in Japan for heating pots and pans: gas stoves and induction cooktops. Gas produces a flame of over 1800°F (1000°C) that transfers heat to the oil through the pot. Traditionally, tempura pots are made of iron, aluminum, copper, or bronze (usually a copper-tin alloy).

Iron pots

Able to withstand intense heat and heavy use, iron pots do not heat up easily, but do not cool down easily either. Iron rusts quickly if not cared for properly.

Aluminum pots

Widely used for cooking because aluminum is light, rust-resistant and conducts heat well.

Bronze pots

These are generally made of an alloy of about 90 percent copper and 10 percent tin. This type of pot conducts heat very easily and is popular for its beautiful golden color.

If using an induction cooktop, you must use a pot made of a compatible material, such as iron or enameled iron. Aluminum pots generally cannot be used.

The pots used at Tempura Nakagawa are made of cast aluminum. Casting refers to a method where metal is melted and poured into a mold to form the pot. The pot takes advantage of aluminum's properties — quick to heat and quick to cool — allowing for delicate temperature control in a single pot while frying. The pot shown has an inner diameter of 15 inches (39 cm), and is 4 inches (10 cm) high and ¼ inch (5 mm) thick.

The Science of Pots and Other Tools

Selecting the right materials

To ensure that the tempura batter and ingredients both achieve the right finish, it is important to control the temperatures of the oil and the batter. The thermal conductivity of the pot the tempura is fried in, as well as the container in which the batter is made, have great influence on the temperature of the oil and batter.

The temperature of a pot differs greatly between the areas where it is exposed to a gas flame and the areas where it is not. Uneven pot temperature leads directly to uneven oil temperature. To maintain a consistent frying-oil temperature, it's essential to first minimize temperature variation in the pot itself. Pots made from materials with high thermal conductivity, such as copper or aluminum, distribute heat quickly and evenly, which helps prevent temperature inconsistencies.

To make a light, delicate batter, it's important not to produce too much gluten (see page 81). This requires keeping the batter at a low temperature. When the temperature of the batter is high, the molecular movements of gliadin and glutenin are more intense and they tend to become entangled with each other, resulting in the formation of more gluten. But if the temperature of the batter is low, the gliadin and glutenin do not become so entangled and the gluten does not increase as much. If a ceramic or heat-resistant glass container with low thermal conductivity is used for the batter, this helps maintain the batter's low temperature. These materials prevent outside heat from affecting the batter and also reduce heat loss from the batter, helping keep it consistently cool.

Thermal Conductivity (by Material)

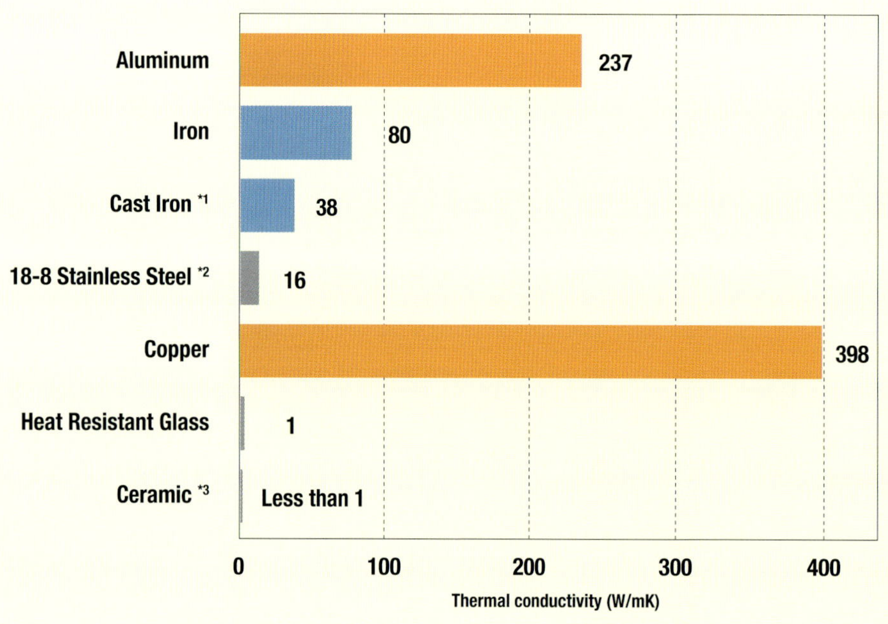

*1. Made by mixing in more than 20% carbon to increase the strength of the iron.

*2. A general term for corrosion-resistant alloy steels, mainly steel combined with chromium, or with both nickel and chromium. The numbers 18-8 indicate that it contains 18% chromium and 8% nickel. This is the standard type of stainless steel.

*3. A typical example is an earthenware dish such as the Japanese donabe.

Source: Hidemi Sato, *Oishisa o tsukuru netsu no kagaku* (*The Science of Heat for Delicious Flavor)*, Shibata Shoten, 2007.

Dimensions of the pot used for deep-frying

The thickness and shape of the pot as well as the material it is made with affect the temperature of the oil in it. The thicker the pot, the more heat it can retain within its body. Even if the oil temperature drops sharply when ingredients are added, a thick pot can quickly bring the oil temperature back up using the heat it has stored. In addition, if the pot is deep, it can hold more oil. The more oil you use, the more heat is stored in the oil itself, so its temperature does not drop as much when the ingredients are added.

However, it is often said that the amount of tempura ingredients placed in the oil should not exceed one-third of the oil's surface area. This is because too many ingredients at once not only lower the oil temperature, but also make it harder for moisture evaporating from the batter to escape. In a pot with a wide opening, the oil's surface area is larger, which means you can add more ingredients at once compared to a narrower pot.

The Ideal Tempura Pot

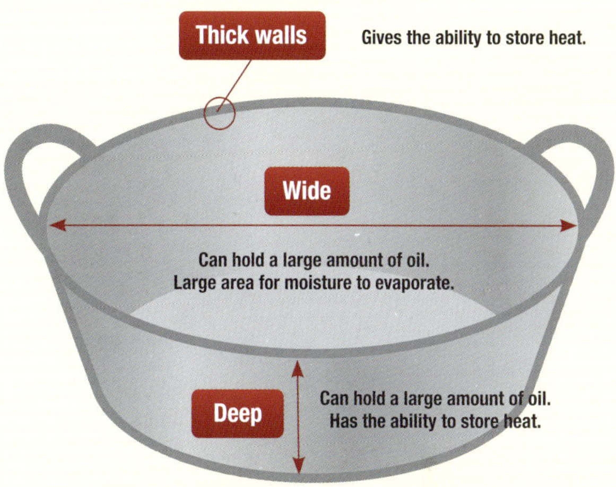

Konabashi chopsticks

The chopsticks used to make the tempura batter are called *konabashi* (see page 35).They are much thicker than the usual cooking chopsticks you see in Japanese kitchens. To prevent the formation of gluten, the flour and water are not stirred together when mixing; instead the mixture is lightly tapped from above with the konabashi chopsticks. The thicker the chopsticks the easier it is to perform that tapping motion, and the flour and water will blend well together. If the chopsticks are thin like regular cooking chopsticks, it is difficult to mix the flour and water just by tapping, so you end up stirring. But stirring causes gliadin and glutenin to move and entangle as they're pulled along by the chopsticks, which leads to excessive gluten formation.

道具

Kitchen Equipment

Here is the equipment you need to make the ideal tempura. For each process – including sifting the flour; mixing the flour, eggs and water; and draining the oil from the deep-fried tempura – it is important to have the right tools.

キッチンポット

Stainless Steel Container

This is used for holding the egg mixture. Use stainless steel (page 32), which conducts heat less easily. This container is about 4 inches (10.5 cm) diameter and 4 inches (10 cm) high.

粉ふるい

Flour Sifter (*konafurui*)

The flour is sifted in advance using a flour sifter. This removes any lumps while also incorporating air, which helps the tempura fry up light and crispy. This sifter is 5½ inches (14.5 cm) in diameter and 2¼ inches (6 cm) high.

ホイッパー

Whisk

Eggs have a high viscosity and are often described as having elasticity or body. To make it easier to combine the egg mixture with flour, the elasticity of the eggs is thoroughly broken down using a whisk. This whisk is 12 inches (30 cm) long.

粉鉢

Batter Bowl (*konabachi*)
A large bowl for making tempura batter. The batter must be kept cold to prevent gluten formation. To minimize heat transfer, a ceramic bowl with low thermal conductivity is used. A flat bottom can cause chopsticks to catch while mixing, so this custom-made bowl from Tempura Nakagawa has a rounded base. This bowl is 12 inches (30 cm) in diameter, 1 inch (3 cm) thick and 7 inches (17.5 cm) high.

粉箸

Flour-mixing Chopsticks (*konabashi*)
These chopsticks are thicker than the usual long cooking chopsticks often seen in Japanese kitchens. They are well suited for combining the flour and water by tapping rather than stirring, so that gluten does not form. These chopsticks are 13 inches (33 cm) long and ½ inch (1.5 cm) thick.

A well-used pair of flour-mixing chopsticks
These flour-mixing chopsticks have been used for a long time. The areas where batter tends to stick have been carefully washed over time, causing noticeable indentations.

鉢

Small Bowl (*hachi*)

This bowl is used to add flour and eggs to the base batter to achieve the idea consistency. Use a ceramic bowl that fits snugly in your hand and does not transfer heat easily. This bowl is 6 inches (15 cm) in diameter and 3 inches (8 cm) high.

菜箸

Bamboo Cooking Chopsticks (*saibashi*)

For frying the tempura, use lightweight bamboo cooking chopsticks that fit well in your hand. These chopsticks are 17½ inches (45 cm) long and ½ inch (1 cm) thick.

まな箸

Metal Serving Chopsticks (*manabashi*)

These are used for arranging food on the serving dish. At Tempura Nakagawa, they are used for cutting the conger eel in front of the customer. These chopsticks are 15 inches (38 cm) long and ½ inch (1 cm) thick.

網付きバット

Tray with a Wire Rack (*amitsukibatto*)

To let the deep-fried tempura rest, place the pieces in a tray with a rack to drain off the oil.

揚げ玉とり

Skimmer (*agedamatori*)

Used to scoop out tempura batter crumbs from the oil. This skimmer is 6 inches (15 cm) in diameter and the handle is 8 inches (20 cm) long.

片刃包丁

Single-bevel Knife
(*kataba bocho*)

Single-bevel Knife

A single-bevel knife — with the blade sharpened on only one side — is used to prepare fish. By cutting precisely along the fine boundaries where bone meets flesh and skin meets flesh, you can produce clean fillets that retain their flavor and texture even when coated in batter and deep-fried at high temperatures.

No matter how perfectly the batter is prepared, no matter how well-timed the frying is, if the fish has not been properly prepped, you won't get delicious tempura. If there are extra cuts in the flesh or the filleting is rough, the umami will seep out through the uneven surfaces, and since the flesh is already prone to breaking apart when heated, it becomes even more fragile. When prepping fish, use a sharp knife and aim to make as few cuts as possible—cut through in one smooth motion.

At Tempura Nakagawa, we use single-bevel knives called *kataba bocho*. Since the blade is only on one side, the knife naturally veers away from the beveled side as it moves forward, producing a slanted cut. When you run the knife along the bone, it instinctively moves away from it, allowing you to glide forward and neatly separate the flesh from the bone.

10 inches (26 cm)

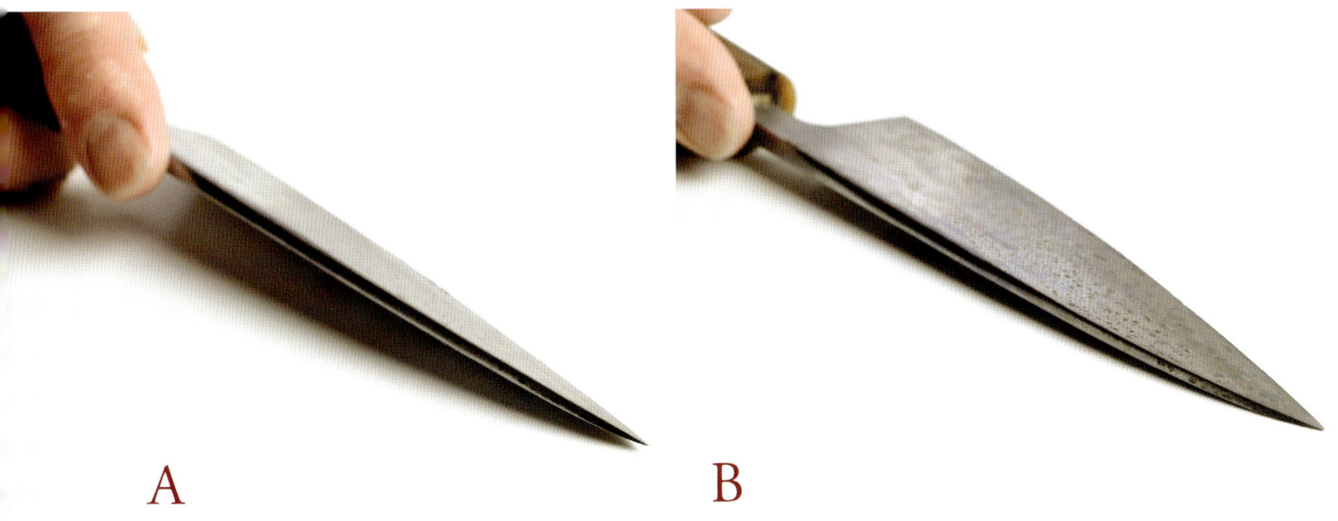

Fish bones are uneven. To avoid leaving excess flesh on the bones, it's important to run the knife along the contours of the bone. As you cut, you'll need to make fine adjustments—tilting the knife upright (A) or laying it down flat (B)—in response to the bumps and hollows of the bones.

Insert the tip of the blade right at the boundary between the bone and the flesh, and cut along it to avoid leaving any meat on the bone. The key is not to grip the knife too tightly – you want to be able to feel how the blade makes contact with the bone through your hand.

CHAPTER 3

INGREDIENT PREPARATION

“Handle fish with respect, and it will reward you with perfect texture.”

—Chef Takashi Nakagawa

Japanese Whiting
(*kisu*)

Japanese Whiting

ORDER: Perciformes **FAMILY:** Sillaginidae **SCIENTIFIC NAME:** Sillago japonica

The fish referred to as *kisu* in tempura is Japanese whiting. The original name is *kisugo*, a common regional term, with the final *go* often dropped. Although it is available year-round, its peak season is May to July.

Total length: 6½ inches (17 cm)

This fish has been caught since the Edo period (1603–1868) in Japan, and is considered an essential ingredient for classic Edomae tempura. Its beautiful shape and translucent white flesh remain soft and plump even after cooking. It is typically butterflied from the back before frying. Because the flesh is delicate and tender, care must be taken not to damage the skin when scaling—avoid scraping repeatedly with the knife. Since tempura is a cooking method that seals in the flavor of the fish by coating it in batter and frying at high temperature, it's crucial to thoroughly remove any fishy-smelling scales, innards, and blood.

How to butterfly whiting

Insert the knife from the back and open up the fish. As you cut, run the blade along the backbone to avoid leaving any flesh behind on the bones.

1 Place the fish with its belly facing you and hold it by the head to avoid transferring body heat. Starting from the tail, move the knife toward the head to scale one side of the fish.

How to Fry Japanese Whiting ➡ page 128

2 Move the knife gently so that you do not damage the skin.

3 There are scales on the belly too, so draw the knife gently along it.

4 Insert the knife diagonally near the gills on the head. Don't cut off the head at this stage.

5 Place the back of the fish to face you and move the knife from the tail toward the head to remove the scales.

6 Insert the knife diagonally into the gills on the head.

7 Place the fish with the belly side facing you, and cut off the head along the diagonal cuts you made earlier into both gills. Pull out the guts at the same time.

8 Place the fish with its back facing you, lay the knife flat, and cut along the backbone, keeping the blade closely aligned with the backbone as you go.

9 Try not to leave any flesh on the bone as you cut through.

10 As you cut, gently lift the upper fillet little by little in sync with your progress, guiding the knife gradually toward the belly while staying close to the backbone.

11 Holding the upper part of the fish, cut along the bone to the very end of the belly where the upper and lower parts are connected.

12 Flip the fish so the skin faces up, lay the knife flat, and insert it from the head end. Then cut along the bones, working your way toward the tail.

13 Leave the tail on and just cut off the bony section.

14 Cut off the back fin.

15 Trim away the belly bones on one side.

16 Trim off the belly bones on the other side as well. Rinse the fish with water and pat dry. ➡ page 128

穴子

Conger Eel
(*anago*)

Total length: 17 inches (43 cm)

Conger Eel

ORDER: Anguilliformes **FAMILY:** Congridae
SCIENTIFIC NAME: Conger myriaster

A saltwater fish that spends all its life in the sea. Its body is mostly brown, with a paler, whitish underside. A row of white spots runs along each side of its body.

Most conger eel live in coastal and inner bay waters shallower than 300 feet (100 meters); during the day they hide in the shade of rocks or in sand and mud. The conger eel has no scales and its surface is slimy. Many restaurants purchase conger eels that have already been killed and prepared by eel specialists. When prepping them, a skewer is used to secure the head, and the fish is split open. It's important to fillet the eel quickly in a single motion, as extra cuts not only ruin the shape but also cause the umami to escape. To prevent any fishy smell, the innards and blood are carefully scraped out and thoroughly cleaned. When frying, the eel is typically cooked whole.

How to Fry Conger Eel ➡ page 134

Butterflying from the back

Conger eel is opened from the back—this is called *sebiraki* (back-opening). The knife is inserted from the back, and the fish is opened into a single piece while keeping the belly side intact. The opposite is *harabiraki* (belly-opening), where the knife is inserted from the belly side. Belly-opening is more common in the Osaka region, while back-opening is typical in the Tokyo area. Once you get used to it, butterflying an eel takes less than 15 seconds.

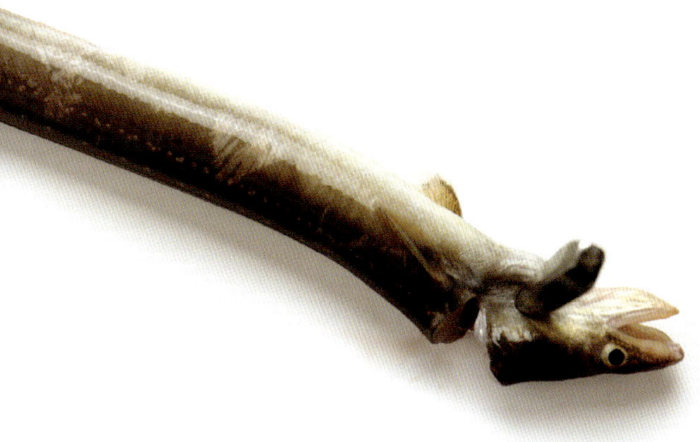

1 With the back facing you, secure the eel to the cutting board by driving a skewer between the eye and the gill.

2 Hold the eel down with your left hand, and insert the knife from the side of the gill.

3 When the knife hits the backbone, tilt the spine of the knife slightly toward the head, angle the blade, and quickly move it toward the tail, cutting along the backbone.

4 To avoid cutting through the belly skin, guide the blade along the edge of the backbone as you continue slicing.

5 Cut along the backbone. Be mindful of the blade angle as you work, so that you don't accidentally sever the bone.

6 With your left hand, gently pull the eel to create tension as you cut along the backbone. Once you reach the area of the anus, draw the knife through in one swift motion.

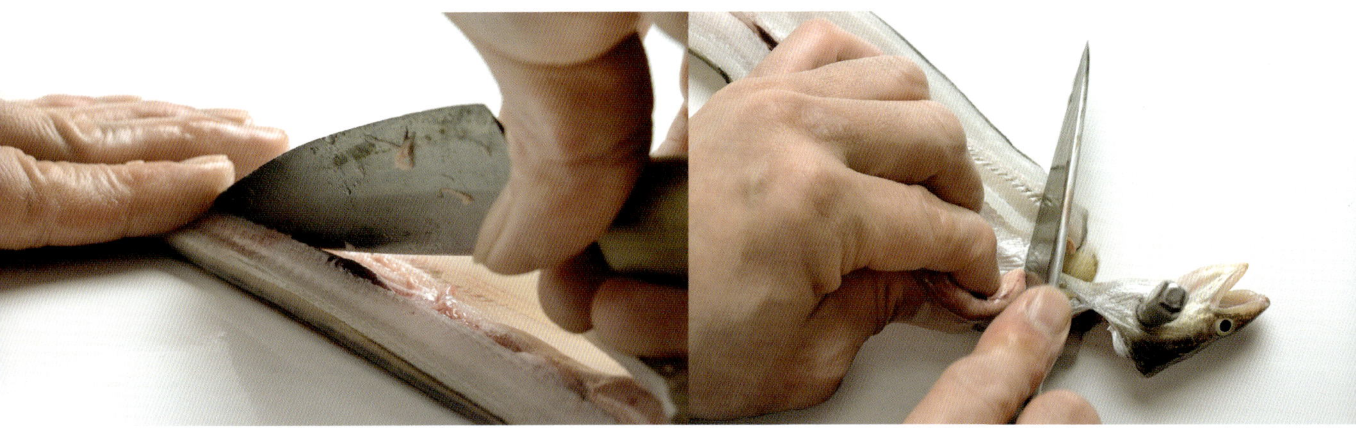

7 Open up the body of the eel with the tip of the knife. Hold the knife with the blade facing upward, insert the tip at the end of the gut area near the tail, and make a cut along the side of the backbone toward the tail — being careful not to cut through the bottom skin.

8 Make a slit from the head side of the guts. Lay the knife flat along the surface.

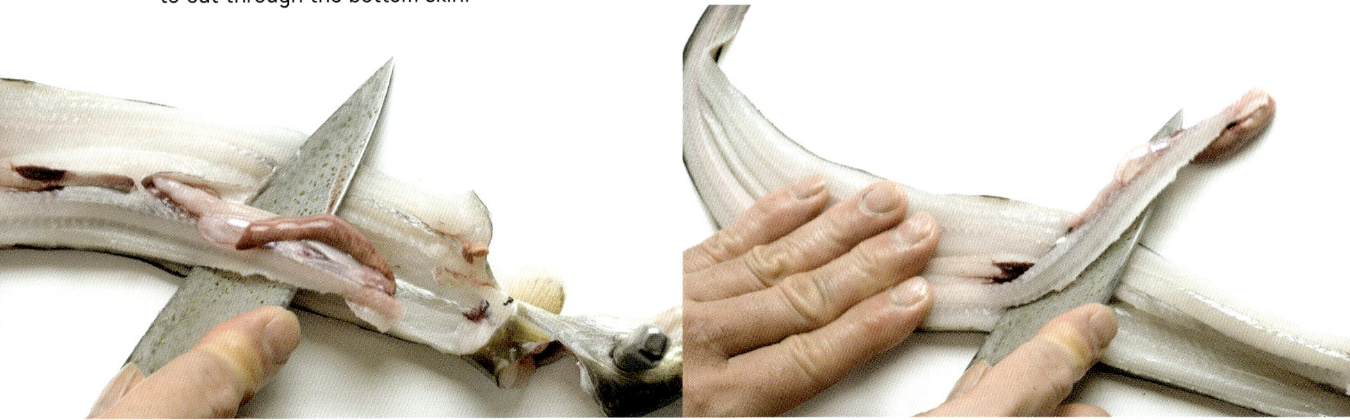

9 Lay the knife flat along the lower edge of the backbone and continue cutting, slicing through the backbone and guts together as you go.

10 Keep on cutting toward the tail.

11 Continue cutting to separate the bone from the flesh at the tail end, then cut off the head. Use the tip of the knife to carefully remove any remaining innards from the flesh.

Head, bones and innards

This is what is left after preparation. Since the knife is run along the edges of the head, bones and innards, there are almost no traces of these parts on the flesh.

目鯒

Big-eyed Flathead (*megochi*)

Big-eyed Flathead

ORDER: Perciformes **FAMILY:** Zippidae **SCIENTIFIC NAME:** Suggrundus meerdervoortii

This fish is characterized by its flat head, which looks as if it has been squashed. It lives in sandy areas and is fished all over Japan except around the northernmost main island of Hokkaido. It has various names in different regions.

Big-eyed flathead is at its most delicious when prepared as tempura. Its slimy skin has a slight odor, but rather than removing all the slime, leaving some of it enhances the aroma. The flesh is firm, with a mild flavor that carries a rich, distinctive umami. Because of its uniquely flat head and body shape, the fish is turned over and cut from the belly side, keeping the body attached at the base of the tail and arranged into a pine-needle shape. You can leave the skin on or remove it, but keeping the skin allows the flavor of the fat between the skin and flesh to shine through. Since the flesh is thick, a cut is made down the center of the fillet—leaving the skin intact—to ensure even cooking of the meat.

Total length:
8 inches (21 cm)

How to Fry Big-eyed Flathead ➡ page 156

Telling Males and Females Apart

The male fish has a dark-edged anal fin, while females have a lighter, whitish edge. There is almost no difference in taste between them.

Preparing a big-eyed flathead

Wash off the slime on the surface of the fish in a bowl of salt water that is about the same as seawater (3 percent salt concentration).

1 Hold the big-eyed flathead with the belly side facing up, and place the knife blade along the bottom edge of the head.

2 Make a diagonal cut into the head side.

3 Cut off the head.

4 Position the fish with the head side on the right and the belly side facing toward you. Lay the knife flat and cut toward the backbone from the head side.

5 Stop cutting just before you reach the tail. The tail is not cut off.

6 Place the fish with the head side on the right and the back side facing toward you. Lay the knife flat and cut toward the backbone from the head side.

7 Stop cutting just before you reach the tail. The two sides of the fillet should remain connected at the tail end.

8 With the flesh side facing up, make a reverse cut down the center, leaving just a single layer of skin intact. ➡ page 156

墨烏賊

Golden Cuttlefish

ORDER: Sepiidae **FAMILY:** Sepiidae **SCIENTIFIC NAME:** Sepia esculenta

A fin runs along the entire length of the side. Between the dorsal muscles and the internal organs, there is a shell-like structure enclosed in a thin membrane.

Golden Cuttlefish (*sumi-ika*)

The squid used for tempura varies by season: bigfin reef squid (*aori-ika*), see page 58, is used in summer, and golden cuttlefish (*sumi-ika*) in winter. Golden cuttlefish, also known as *ko-ika,* has an internal shell (cuttlebone). If you were to distinguish them by their qualities, bigfin reef squid is prized for its flavor, while golden cuttlefish is valued for its texture. To bring out its dense, sticky mouthfeel, the thin membranes on both the inner and outer surfaces of the flesh are carefully removed.

Total length:
12 inches (30 cm)

How to Fry Golden Cuttlefish ➡ page 130

How to Prepare Golden Cuttlefish

Beneath the outer skin and on the inner surface of the flesh, there is a thin membrane. If this membrane is left intact, it can cause the oil to splatter and the texture to become tough when heated, making it difficult to bite through. Carefully removing it is key.

1 Press down just above the eyes of the cuttlefish with both thumbs to push out the cuttlebone inside the body.

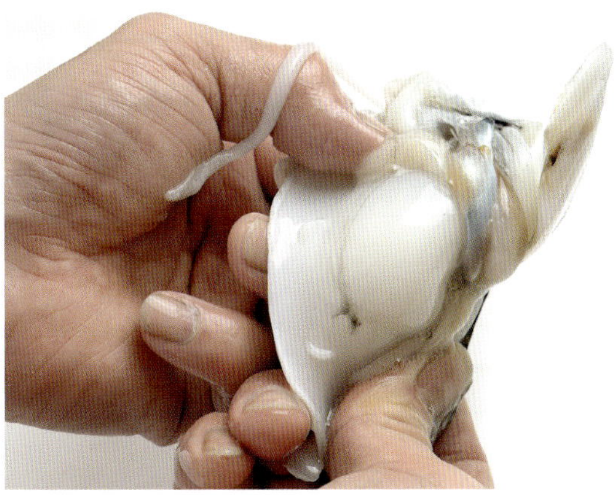

2 Carefully pull out the tentacles and innards, being sure not to break the ink sac. While pushing out the cuttlebone, peel off the inner membrane as well. Remove the cuttlebone.

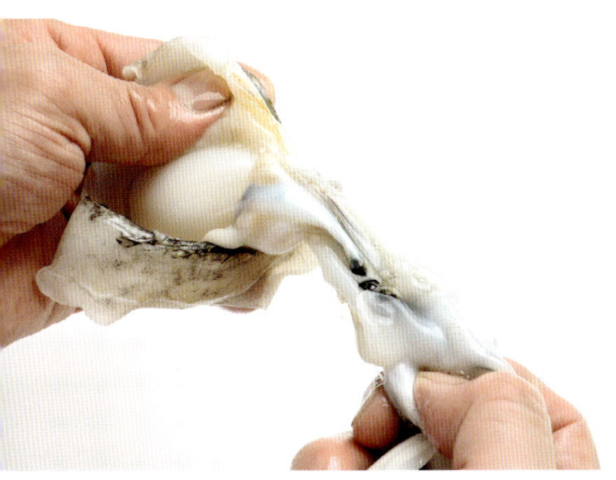

3 Carefully pull out the tentacles and innards, making sure not to break the ink sac.

4 Then, while pushing out the cuttlebone, peel away the inner membrane. Remove the cuttlebone. Slide your fingers between the flesh and the outer skin, and pull off the surface skin.

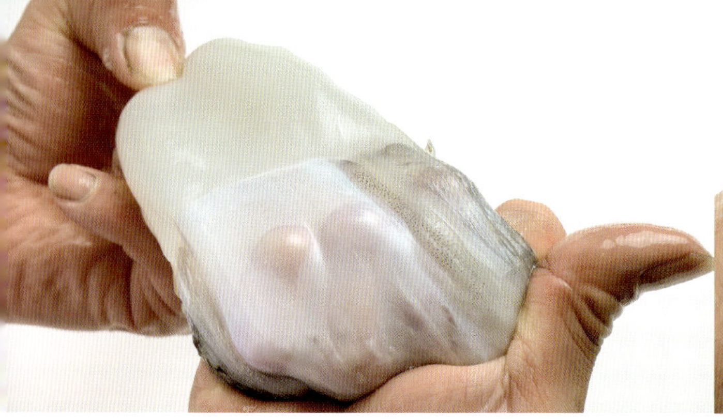

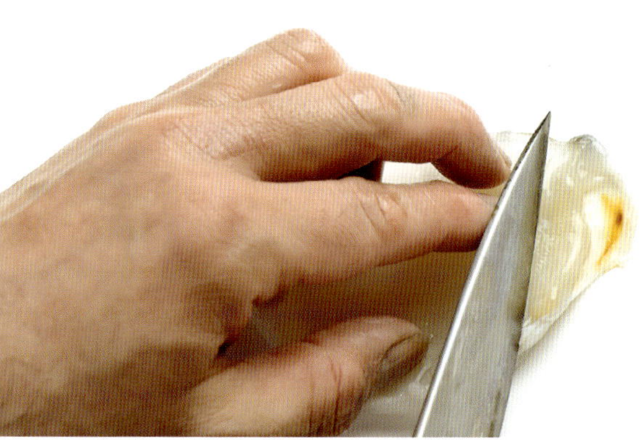

5 Keep pulling to remove the upper skin.

6 Cut off the guts that are attached to the body.

7 Cut away the inner cartilage.

8 Use a skewer or pick to remove the thin inner membrane.

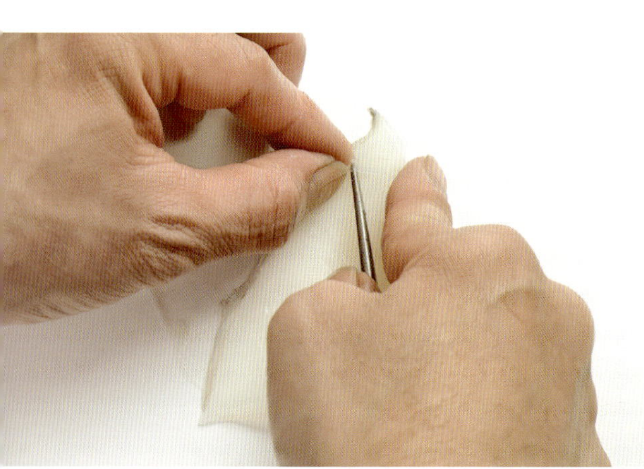

9 Insert a skewer or pick at the edge of the thin outer membrane.

10 Grip the spot where the pick was inserted, and peel off the membrane in one smooth motion. ➡ page 130

すみいか
きす

障泥烏賊

Bigfin Reef Squid
(*aori-ika*)

Bigfin Reef Squid

ORDER: Tricoplaciformes **FAMILY:** Squamata
SCIENTIFIC NAME: Sepioteuthis lessoniana

A member of the Japanese flying squid family, this squid does not have a carapace. It is known for its large, gracefully rippling fins and the beautiful emerald green coloration next to its eyes.

The king of squid from spring to summer is the *aori-ika*, or bigfin reef squid. Its name comes from *aori*, a type of mudguard that hangs down from both sides of a horse to keep its belly from getting splashed. The squid was given this name because its broad side fins resemble those flaps.

When it swims, its body appears beautifully translucent, which is why it's also called *mizu-ika*, or "water squid." It's known for its thick flesh, rich umami flavor, and smooth, almost creamy texture.

Total length:
29½ inches (75 cm)
Body: 15½ inches (40 cm)

How to Fry Bigfin Reef Squid ➡ page 132

How to Prepare Bigfin Reef Squid

Removing the outer skin and then carefully peeling off the thin membrane underneath is an important step common to all squid, but with bigfin reef squid, the membrane is especially difficult to remove, so extra care is needed. Once the body is opened, make a shallow cut with a knife and peel the membrane from both sides toward the center.

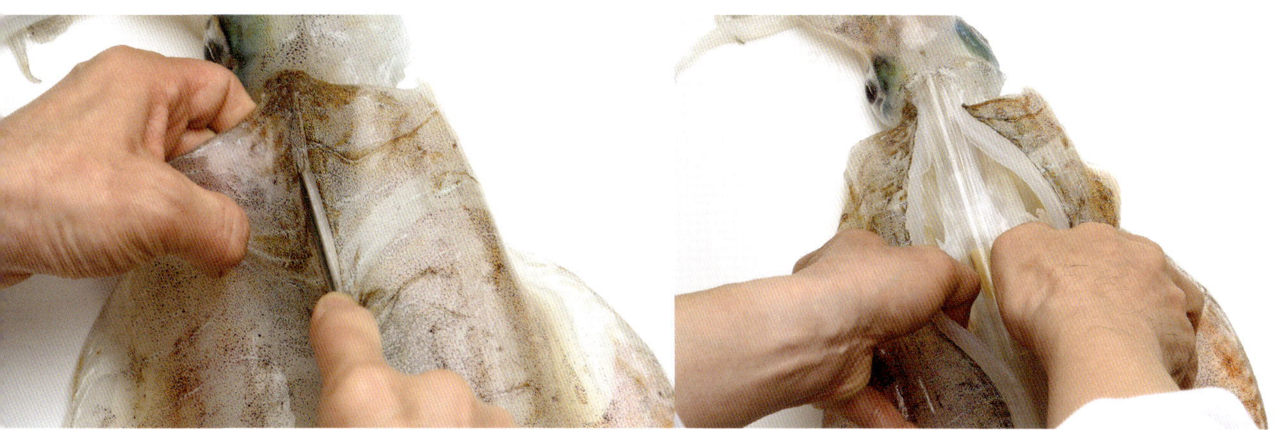

1 Make a straight vertical cut down the body with a knife, cutting just deep enough to reach the cartilage. Grasp the tentacles and pull out the innards and cartilage.

2 Use your hands to open the cut sides outward.

3 Grasp the tentacles and pull out the innards and cartilage.

4 Place the opened body with the inner (organ) side facing up and the tip pointing toward you. Slide your fingers between the skin and the flesh, and peel off the outer skin in one swift motion.

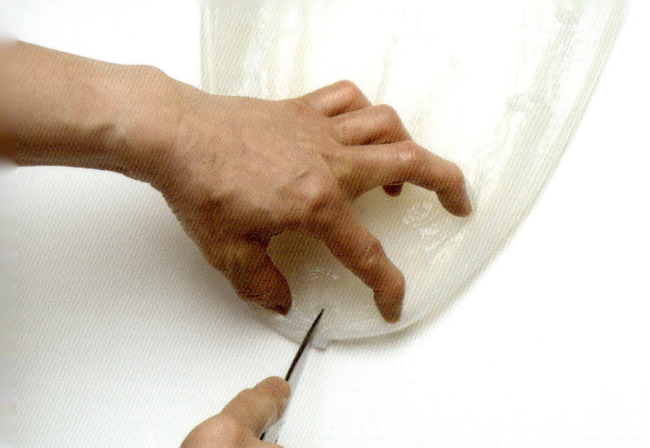

5 Place the opened body with the inner (organ) side facing up and the tip toward you. Make a cut at the tip.

6 Cut off the ½ inch (1 cm) wide strips of cartilage along both sides of the body. Place the opened body with the inner (organ) side facing up and the tip pointing away from you.

7 Trim off the two pieces of cartilage attached near the lower part of the body.

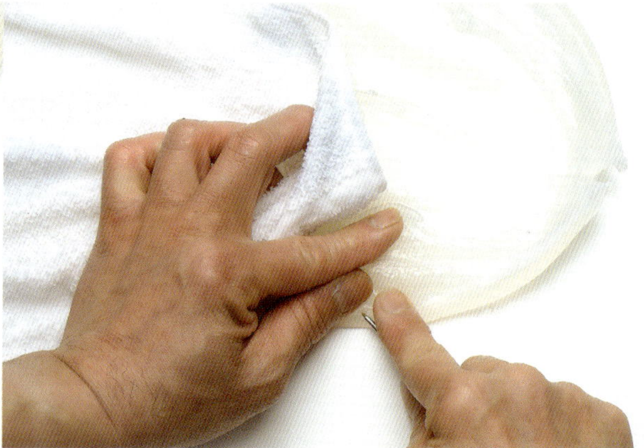

8 Place the inner (organ) side facing up with the tip on the right. Press a cloth over it and peel off the thin membrane.

9 Finally, use your thumbs to peel off the remaining thin membrane upward from the center. Remove all of the thin membrane completely.

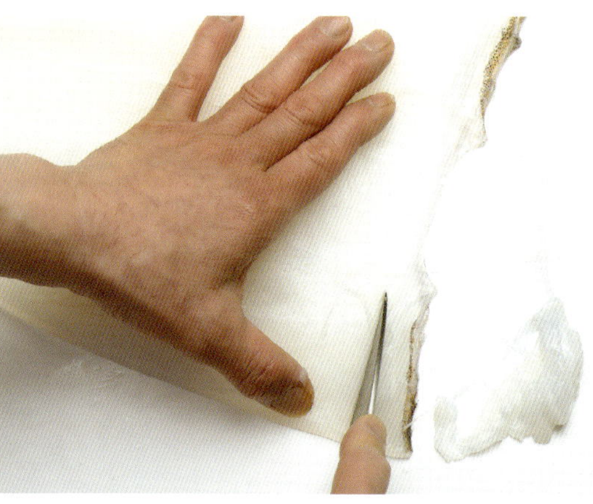

10 Make a cut about ½ inch (1 cm) from the bottom edge of the body, leaving the outer skin intact. At both ends, cut all the way through, without leaving the outer skin.

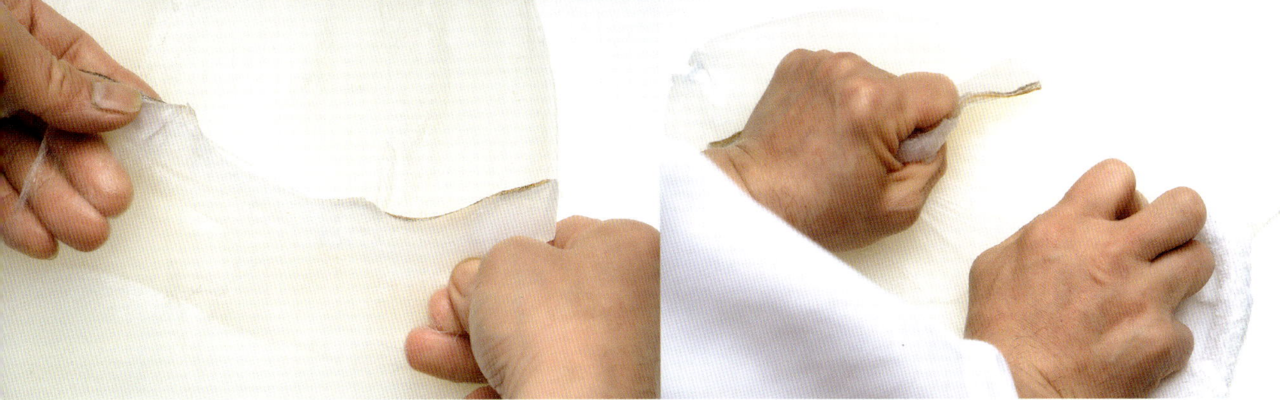

11 Peel off the outer thin membrane as well. Place the squid with the tip pointing upward, press a cloth over it, and grip the membrane at the cut on the lower left. Pull it toward the center and peel off about one-third of it.

12 Peel in the same way from the lower right. Finally, use your thumbs to peel off all the remaining thin membrane upward from the center. ➡ page 132

TECHNIQUE FOCUS

Removing the membrane and severing the fibers

To make tender squid tempura, carefully peel the skin and membrane without leaving any thin layers, and then cut the flesh into thin strips crosswise, severing the fibers.

The membrane of the bigfin reef squid is said to be especially hard to peel off. There are several methods for removing the membrane, but at Tempura Nakagawa, knife cuts are made on the left and right sides of the body (see diagram, right) and the membrane is peeled toward the center. By doing this the membrane is less liable to tear and easier to peel.

Make ½ inch (1 cm) long cuts on either side of the body.

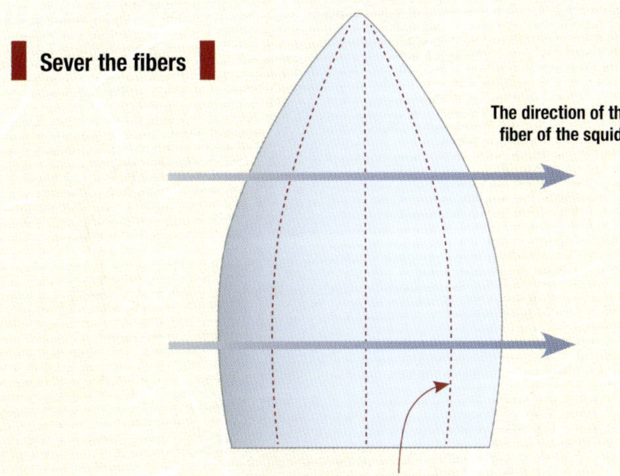

The Science of Seafood Muscles

Seafood used for tempura is divided into vertebrates, which have a backbone, and invertebrates, which do not have a backbone. In general fish are vertebrates, while shrimp (arthropods and crustaceans), squid and shellfish (mollusks) are invertebrates. Vertebrates have an internal skeleton (endoskeleton) that supports the body through a series of connected bones. These bones are connected to muscles inside the body, and the muscles move the bones.

Invertebrates, by contrast, possess what are called obliquely striated muscles, which are not found in vertebrates. In shrimp, these muscles are attached to the outer skeleton (exoskeleton) and are used to move the body. Squid have no bones at all and rely entirely on obliquely striated muscles for movement.

Vertebrates

The Muscles of Fish

The flesh of fish used for tempura is made up of muscle. Muscle consists of long, slender cells called muscle fibers, which are bundled together by collagen membranes. These bundles of muscle fibers are then grouped into larger bundles, also wrapped in collagen membranes. Each muscle fiber is composed of long, thread-like myofibrillar proteins and small, globular sarcoplasmic proteins. The sarcoplasmic proteins are water-soluble and have a soft, gel-like consistency, filling the spaces between the myofibrillar proteins.

Fish are generally categorized into red-fleshed and white-fleshed varieties, but white-fleshed fish are more commonly used for tempura. Compared to red-fleshed fish, white fish have higher water content and lower fat. They also contain less of the jelly-like sarcoplasmic proteins found in red fish, which makes their flesh softer and more prone to breaking apart, but also easier to flake. In the case of tempura, however, the fish is wrapped in batter, so there is no need to worry about the flesh falling apart, and because the batter contains a good amount of oil, white fish with their lower fat content and mild flavor are generally more suitable than red-fleshed fish.

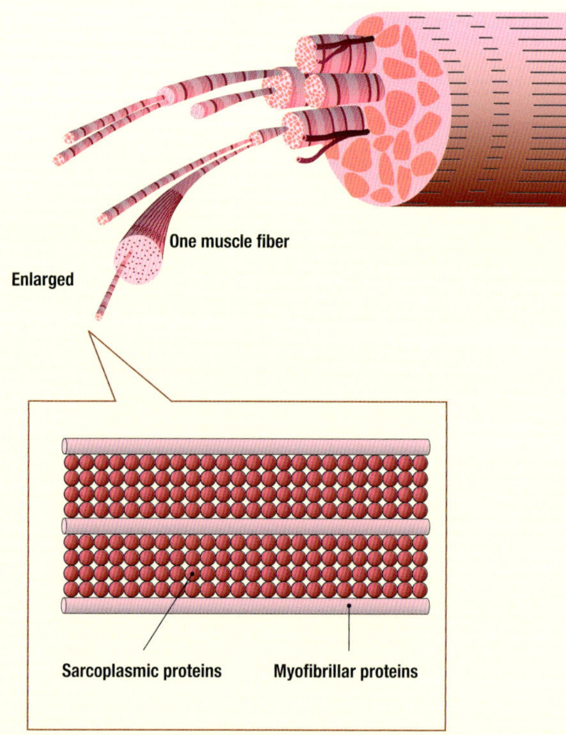

Edomae Fish

Edomae fish—meaning those caught in Tokyo Bay—include conger eel (*anago*), Japanese whiting (*kisu*), big-eyed flathead (*megochi*), tidepool gunnel (*ginpo*), yellowfin goby (*haze*) and Japanese icefish (*shirauo*). Most of these fish live on the seafloor, and usually do not move around much, so do not need a lot of oxygen for exercising their muscles. On the other hand, migratory red fish need oxygen to keep their muscles moving as they continue to swim. Red fish store oxygen in a red pigment called myoglobin, which is why their flesh appears red. In the Edo period (1603–1868), red fish such as tuna were considered inferior. One possible reason is that red-fleshed fish often come from the open sea, and it would have taken time to transport them to the Nihonbashi fish market after they were caught. ➡ page 138

If You Break Down Muscle

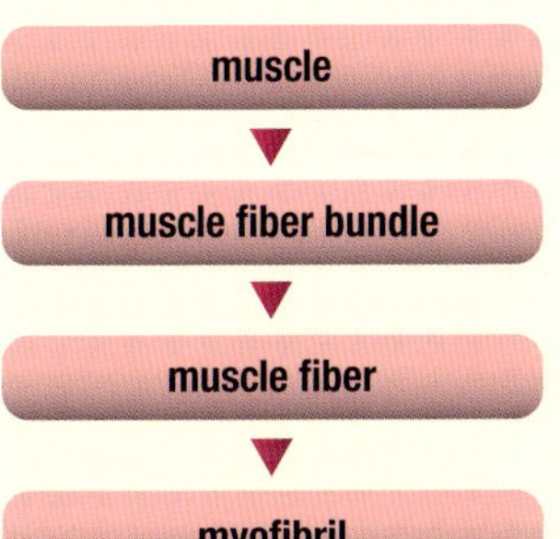

Invertebrates

The Muscles of Shrimp

Shrimp are invertebrates, so their bodies are supported not by an inner backbone, but by a number of tough shells outside their bodies. Inside each shell are muscles, and the muscles attached to the shell contract and relax to enable movement. The muscles attached to the shell in the abdominal region consist of bundles of muscle fibers, a feature characteristic of invertebrates. These bundles are slightly offset and layered on top of one another, forming a twisted structure. The bundles are further supported by other muscles with different shapes in the vertical, horizontal, and cross-sectional planes. The shrimp's signature springy, bouncy texture when cooked comes from this intricate muscle structure—it's a result of repeatedly biting through these tightly packed, twisting bundles of muscle.

Shrimp Muscle Structure

Invertebrates

The Muscles of Squid and Cuttlefish

The meat of the squid or cuttlefish used for tempura is called the mantle, which is the muscle of the body. On the outside of the mantle are four layers of collagen skin. The fourth layer of skin, which adheres to the squid's flesh, is made of tough collagen fibers that run parallel to the direction of the squid's body. The mantle muscle is made up of circular muscles that run in parallel rings perpendicular to the body's axis, and radial muscles that support of the circular ones.

The squid's color comes from pigment cells located between the first and second layers of skin. When the thin skin is carefully peeled by hand, it separates between the second and third layers, removing the pigment cells and making the squid's flesh appear white. Removing the thin skin thoroughly helps create the distinctive texture of squid tempura—springy yet tender.

The reason squid curls up into a boat shape when heated is because the collagen in the fourth layer of skin shrinks. This layer almost always remains even when the skin is peeled in the usual way. However, if all four layers of skin are completely removed, the squid flesh may shrink during cooking, but it will no longer curl or bend.

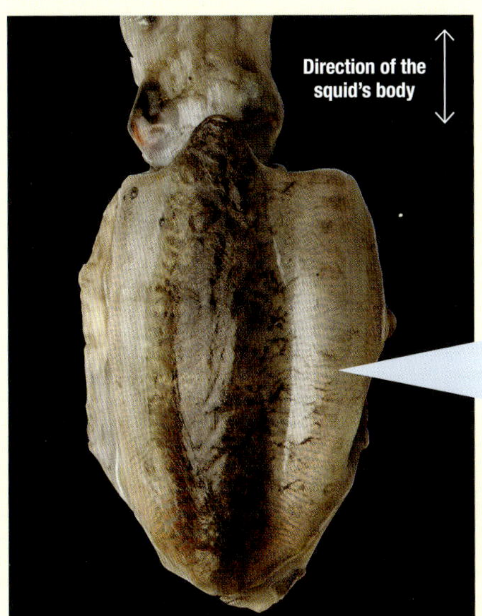

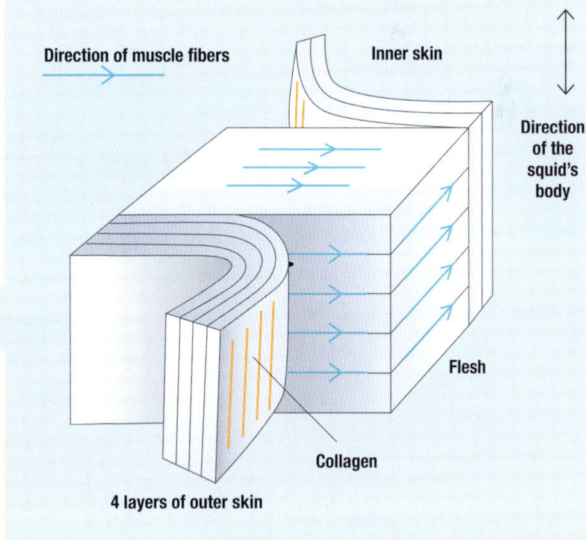

Careful peeling of the squid skin creates the soft, bouncy texture of squid tempura.

Abalone
(*awabi*)

Abalone

ORDER: Lepetellida **FAMILY:** Haliotidae **SCIENTIFIC NAME:** Haliotis discus discus

A type of marine snail. Many species of abalone live in Japan, but their numbers have declined dramatically due to environmental destruction and overfishing.

The abalone is the king of shellfish. It appears as a seasonal tempura delicacy only during the summer months. In Japan, four main types are commonly known: black abalone (*kuro-awabi*), northern abalone (*ezo-awabi*), giant abalone (*madaka-awabi*), and disk abalone (*megai-awabi*). Among these, black abalone is considered the finest. It has a rich, sweet umami flavor and a distinctively firm, crunchy texture. This crunchiness comes from collagen: the more collagen a part contains, the firmer and more resilient it is to the bite. The amount of collagen varies by part of the abalone, with the central portion containing less—making it the softer part.

4¾ inches (12 cm) x
3 inches (8 cm)

How to Fry Abalone ➡ page 162

1 Rub on salt, and rinse the surface well under running water.

2 Insert a spatula (here the handle of a grater is used) between the shell and the body.

3 The spatula will come into contact with the adductor muscle. Push the spatula firmly along the inside of the shell to detach the muscle, then remove the flesh completely.

4 Carefully separate the flesh by hand, taking care not to break the liver.

5 Carefully detach the liver from the flesh by hand, making sure not to break it.

6 Cut off the mouth of the abalone (the red part). ➡ page 162

Yellowfin Goby

Yellowfin Goby (*haze*)

ORDER: Gobiiformes **FAMILY:** Gobildae **SCIENTIFIC NAME:** Acanthogobius flavimanus

There are many varieties of goby, but the one mainly used for tempura is the yellowfin goby. Its trademark feature is a long, fox-like face.

Total length: 8 inches (20.5 cm)

Yellowfin goby is a quintessential Edomae fish. In the Edo period (1603–1868) this fish was popular for its light and delicate flesh, and was eaten as sashimi or tempura right after it was caught. However, this type of yellowfin goby was fished strictly in the summer. At Tempura Nakagawa we also use another type of yellowfin goby known as *ketahaze*, caught in fall and winter, when the water temperature drops and the fish go deeper into the water.

Butterflying goby from the back

Make a back cut, leaving the tail intact. Hold the knife lightly so you can feel how it meets the bones through your hand, and carefully separate the flesh while confirming the position of the bones.

1 Cut off the tip of the tail of the yellowfin goby. Remove the scales on the surface from the tail end aiming toward the head end. Make a cut into the head from the back of the side fin. Remove the scales and make a cut into the other side in the same way.

How to Fry Yellowfin Goby ➡ page 152

2 As you cut off the head, use the tip of the knife to remove the internal organs from inside the body.

3 Rinse out the area where the internal organs were attached. With the back side facing you, lay the knife flat and run it along the backbone from the head end, separating the flesh. Don't cut through the belly side.

4 Open up the flesh and make incisions along both sides of the backbone.

5 Place the fish skin side up with the backbone underneath. Insert the knife between the backbone and the flesh, and carefully cut along, keeping the blade aligned with the uneven surface of the backbone.

6 Trim off the dark portion near the head.
➡ page 152

銀宝

Tidepool Gunnel (*ginpo*)

Tidepool Gunnel

ORDER: Zoarcoidei **FAMILY:** Pholidae **SCIENTIFIC NAME:** Pholis nebulosa

The Japanese name for the tidepool gunnel is *ginpo*. Rigor mortis is severe and the fish becomes as stiff as a stick.

Total length: 8 inches (20 cm)

How to Fry Tidepool Gunnel ➡ page 154

This is an ingredient that really shines when it is made into tempura. Although it has lots of tiny bones, these bones add to the pleasing texture of the fish. The dorsal fin is as sharp as a row of needles, so cut it off cleanly. The scales are very small, so leave them on the fish as part of the unique character of tidepool gunnel.

Butterflying a tidepool gunnel from the back side

Hold the knife lightly so you can better feel the contact between the blade and the bones. As you cut, confirm the position of the bones and proceed as if you're slicing through the fine bones. The dorsal fin consists of a row of small spines, so remove it cleanly.

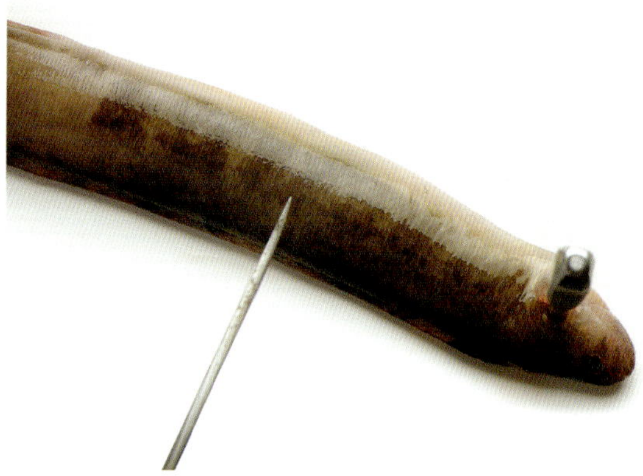

1 With the back side facing you, pierce a skewer through the area near the eyes to secure the fish to the cutting board. Hold the tidepool gunnel firmly with your left hand, and insert the knife at an angle just behind the gill.

2 When the knife touches the backbone, tilt it slightly toward the head, then lay the blade down toward the tail. Keeping the belly skin intact, guide the blade along the edge of the backbone and cut carefully along the bone.

3 Using your left hand, gently pull the flesh as you continue cutting along the backbone. Once you reach the area near the anus, pull the knife through in one motion. Then, cut off the tip of the tail.

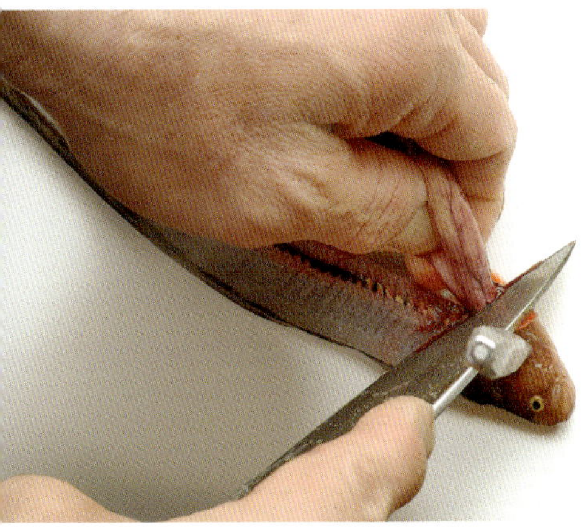

4 Open the flesh and carefully remove the internal organs without breaking them.

5 Insert the knife under the backbone, lay the blade flat along the underside of the bone, and carefully cut forward as if peeling the back-bone away.

6 Cut off the dorsal fin.

7 Cut off the head. ➡ page 154

Ginkgo Nuts

The ginkgo tree is a type of plant called a gymnosperm, which means it doesn't produce true fruits like most trees do. The soft, smelly part of the ginkgo nut isn't actually a fruit – it's the outer layer of the seed. The part we eat is the seed's inner tissue, called the endosperm.

Gingko Nuts
(*ginnan*)

The quintessential autumnal tempura ingredient in Japan is the ginkgo nut. Tempura really makes the most of its sticky mouthfeel and unique bitterness with a hint of sweetness. Carefully remove even the thin inner skin to preserve the delicate texture. Immediately after peeling the skin in hot water, prick the fruit with a toothpick while it is still warm and tender. If there is even a small tear in the nut when frying, the gingko is liable to explode. For skewering, use sturdy, splinter-free wooden toothpicks—something similar in strength to bamboo rather than flimsy party picks.

How to Fry Ginkgo Nuts ➡ page 166

Take care when eating gingko nuts

The unique bitterness of ginkgo nuts is irresistible to those who like them, and people tend to eat too many, which can be bad for you. An early mention of this was in an 1864 culinary text *Hochu biyo wamyo honzo* (Guide to Medicinal and Edible Plants). Ginkgo nuts contain methylpyridoxine, which is toxic to humans. This component is heat-resistant and does not disappear when cooked. The amount that can cause poisoning is estimated to be 7–150 nuts for children and 40–300 nuts for adults. Be careful not to eat too many, and avoid giving them to children under five years of age.

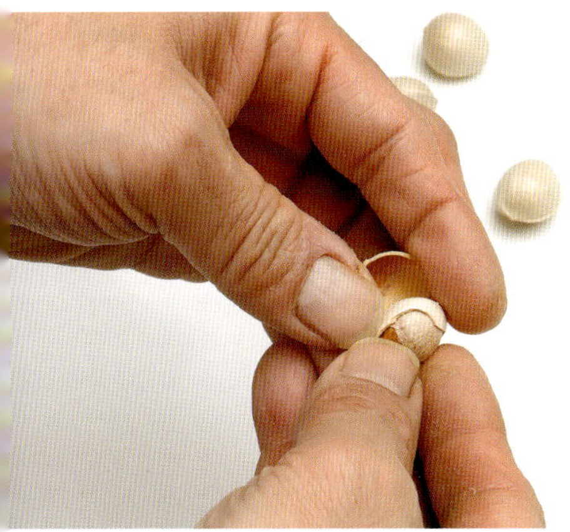

1 Use a small nutcracker or a pair of pliers to gently crack a slit in the shell, then gently peel off.

2 Cover the ginkgo nuts with a little hot water, then gently roll them around with the rounded back of a ladle to remove the thin inner skins.

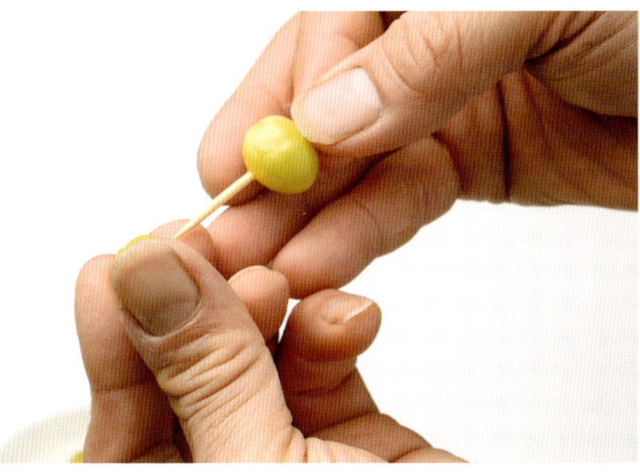

3 Skewer the nuts on a sturdy wooden pick.

4 Skewer 3 nuts on each pick. Place in a container then keep in the refrigerator until you are ready to fry. ➡ page 166

Storing ginkgo nuts

Place shelled gingko nuts in an airtight container, cover with water, put on a lid, and refrigerate. Peel the thin inner skin off in hot water before using (see Step 2, above).

CHAPTER 4

THE BATTER

"Create layers of intensity within a single bowl."

—Chef Takashi Nakagawa

小麦粉

Flour
(*komugiko*)

Flour

Flour is a key ingredient for tempura. Cake or pastry flour – wheat flour with low protein content – is used for the batter, either on its own or combined with egg and water.

When water is added to flour and mixed or kneaded, it becomes sticky. This is due to the formation of gluten (page 80). While some gluten is necessary to give the tempura batter its structure, too much of it prevents moisture and oil from exchanging properly, resulting in a heavy, greasy finish. That's why low-protein cake flour is used for tempura—to limit gluten formation.

To prevent the formation of more gluten than necessary, it is important not to raise the temperature or apply too much force to the batter. For this reason, the ingredients for the batter (eggs, water and flour) must be well chilled. At Tempura Nakagawa, they are refrigerated at least one day before they are used (page 84).

Sift the flour and combine it with the egg and water, and mix with konabashi flour-mixing chopsticks (see page 35), taking care not to overwork the batter.

Dusting with flour

The flour used for dusting acts as an adhesive between the ingredient and the batter. It also absorbs moisture that seeps out from the ingredient, keeping the batter from becoming soggy and helps it fry up crisp. If too much dusting flour is used, it can leave a residue, so be sure to tap off any excess before dipping in the batter.

The Science of Wheat Flour

When moisture is added to flour and kneaded, gluten — a protein unique to flour — is produced (see below). Because the amount of gluten determines the elasticity and texture of wheat-based foods, flours are divided into three categories in Japan: strong, medium, and weak flours, in descending order of protein content. In the United States these are usually called bread, all-purpose and cake or pastry flours respectively.

Strong (bread) flour has a high protein content, producing a large amount of gluten, and is used to make elastic and chewy bread, pasta and dumpling wrappers. Weak (cake or pastry) flour, on the other hand, is low in protein and is used to make fluffy cakes and crispy tempura batter. Medium-strength (all-purpose) flour has a protein content between that of strong and weak flours and is often used in Japan to make such things as udon noodles. Pasta and dumpling wrappers have a variety of textures that can be tailored to suit the needs of the maker and are often made with a blend of weak and strong flours to adjust the elasticity and firmness of the dough.

The Properties of Flour

	Strong flour (bread flour)	Medium flour (all-purpose flour)	Weak flour (cake or pastry flour)
Amount of protein (approximate)	High 11.5–12.5 %	8–9%	6.5–8 % Low
Particle size	Coarse		Fine
Main usages	Pasta, bread, pizza crust, dumpling wrappers, etc.	Udon noodles, other cooking	Tempura batter, cakes and cookies, sauces

What is gluten?

Gluten is formed from two proteins found in wheat flour: gliadin and glutenin. Gliadin is a globular protein with strong stickiness, while glutenin is a strand-like protein with elasticity. When water is added to wheat flour and the dough is kneaded, these two proteins intertwine to form a stretchy, elastic network known as gluten. This gluten-forming process is unique to wheat—other grains like barley, rice and corn do not produce gluten.

The Structure of Gluten

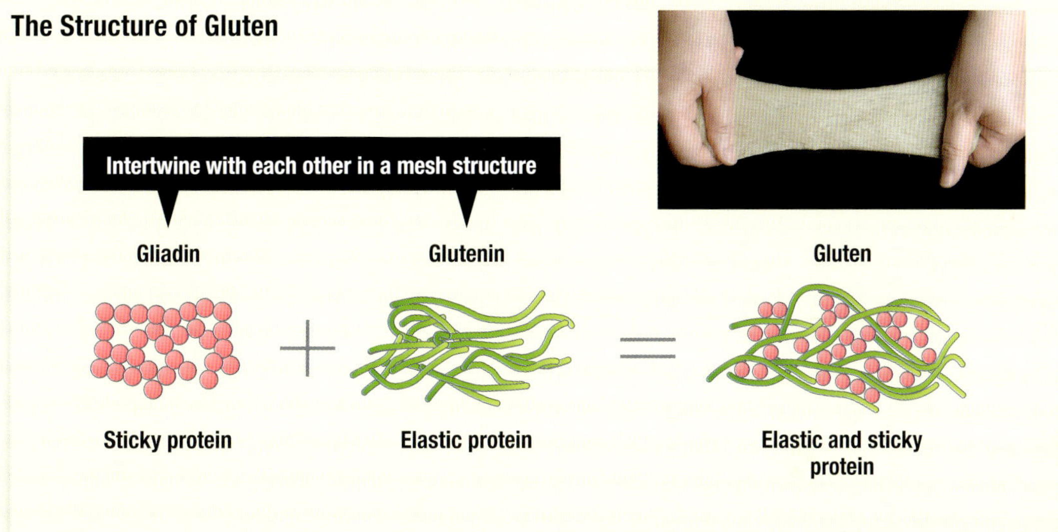

Tempura batter and gluten

Before frying, the moisture in the batter is trapped in the gluten's mesh-like structure. As the tempura is fried, this moisture turns into steam and escapes from the mesh, but if the gluten network is too strong, the steam has a harder time getting out. When too much moisture remains in the batter after frying, the tempura becomes heavy and soggy. The gluten mesh structure becomes stronger the more gluten it contains—that is, the more protein the flour has. For this reason, low-protein cake flour is used for tempura batter. But even when using cake flour, overmixing the flour and water or using ingredients that are too warm also leads to excessive gluten formation, so care is needed (see page 32).

Gluten Mesh Structure

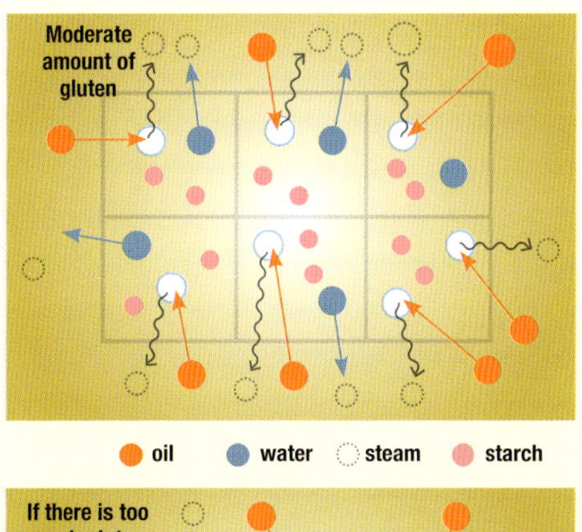

Moisture trapped in the mesh structure is released during frying and replaced by oil.

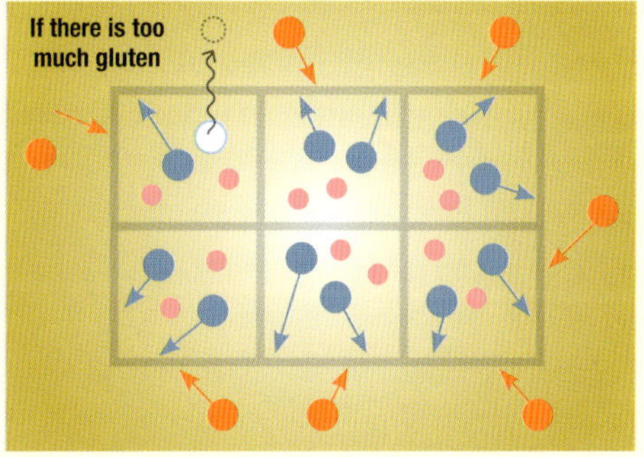

The water trapped in the mesh structure is not released, resulting in a sticky, heavy texture.

Eggs and Water

Although tempura batter can be made by simply mixing water and cake flour, egg is often added to improve the texture and flavor of the batter. The batter base is a combination of egg, water and cake flour, but the proportion of egg can be increased depending on the tempura ingredients.

Eggs & Water (*tamago to mizu*)

Raw egg is a viscous liquid that contains about 75% water. If used as is in tempura batter, it can make the mixture too sticky and overly firm, so the egg is thoroughly beaten and then mixed with water before use.

You'll be familiar with how eggs solidify when boiled or fried, and the same thing happens in hot oil—around 390°F (200°C)—even when the egg is diluted with water. In other words, adding egg helps the batter firm up just enough, which contributes to a crisp texture. To give the coating a bit more firmness, a higher ratio of egg is used for delicate ingredients like cod milt or oysters.

Preparing Tempura Batter

The batter for tempura, made by combining cake flour, egg, and water, hinges most importantly on not developing too much gluten in the flour. The batter at Tempura Nakagawa is of course made with this in mind.

To prevent overdevelopment of gluten in the flour, the temperature of the batter should be low and it should not be overworked. At Tempura Nakagawa, the flour, water and eggs are all refrigerated at least one day in advance. Ice is not used as its state changes as it melts. The flour is placed near the air outlet of the refrigerator, where airflow helps remove moisture.

Whole eggs are used. To avoid overworking the batter, the eggs are well beaten in advance. Then water is added and the mixture is beaten again, and a little less than half the flour required is added and beaten with a tapping motion with a konabashi flour mixing chopsticks (see page 35). The remaining flour is sprinkled on top while holding the chopsticks about halfway down into the batter. This creates areas of thicker and thinner batter within the same bowl. The batter is mixed from the back to the front and from side to side. This creates areas of thicker and thinner batter within the same bowl. In this way, each ingredient can be dipped into the part of the bowl with batter that best suits it. Additional flour or egg is added as needed to fine-tune the mixture.

1 Place the eggs in a bowl and whisk thoroughly until smooth and uniform. Pour the beaten egg into a container.

2 Put water in a bowl, add a little beaten egg and stir to combine. Gradually add more beaten egg as needed, stirring gently with konabashi flour-mixing chopsticks.

3 Hold the chopsticks so they float about halfway down into the bowl, then sift in just under half the necessary amount of cake flour from above using a flour sifter.

4 Stir with a tapping motion using the chopsticks.

5 Sift in more flour.

6 The batter is at the right consistency when you can use the chopsticks to draw a line in the batter that disappears immediately.

7 If needed, sift in more flour to adjust the consistency of the batter.

How to Adjust the Batter

The chilled mixture of cake flour, egg and water makes the base batter. Within the same bowl, areas of thicker and thinner batter are created, allowing the coating to be matched to each ingredient. Depending on the ingredient, additional egg or flour may be added to adjust the consistency.

For ingredients like milt or oysters, adding a little extra egg mixture to the base batter gives it just the right firmness and texture. When the coating fries up crisp, it highlights the soft, creamy texture of the ingredient.

For kakiage — a type of tempura fritter made with chopped vegetables or seafood (see Chapter 7) — transfer some of the base batter to a smaller bowl and add extra egg mixture and flour to make a thicker coating.

Initial state of the batter

Within a single large mixing bowl, areas of thicker and thinner batter are created so the coating can be matched to each ingredient. The batter is adjusted by feel, not using a scale, but below is an example of proportions that were measured on a typical day.

Egg	Water	Weak (cake) flour
55.4°F (13°C) About 2½ oz (70 g)	47.5°F (8.6°C) About 7½ cups (1.7 L)	44.8°F (7.1°C) About 7½ cups (900 g)

Batter Density and Application

The thickness of the batter and the way it is applied varies according to the ingredient. The batter is applied by making instantaneous decisions based on the condition of the ingredients: to dust beforehand with flour or not; to dust with flour on only on one side or both sides; to apply batter thickly or thinly.

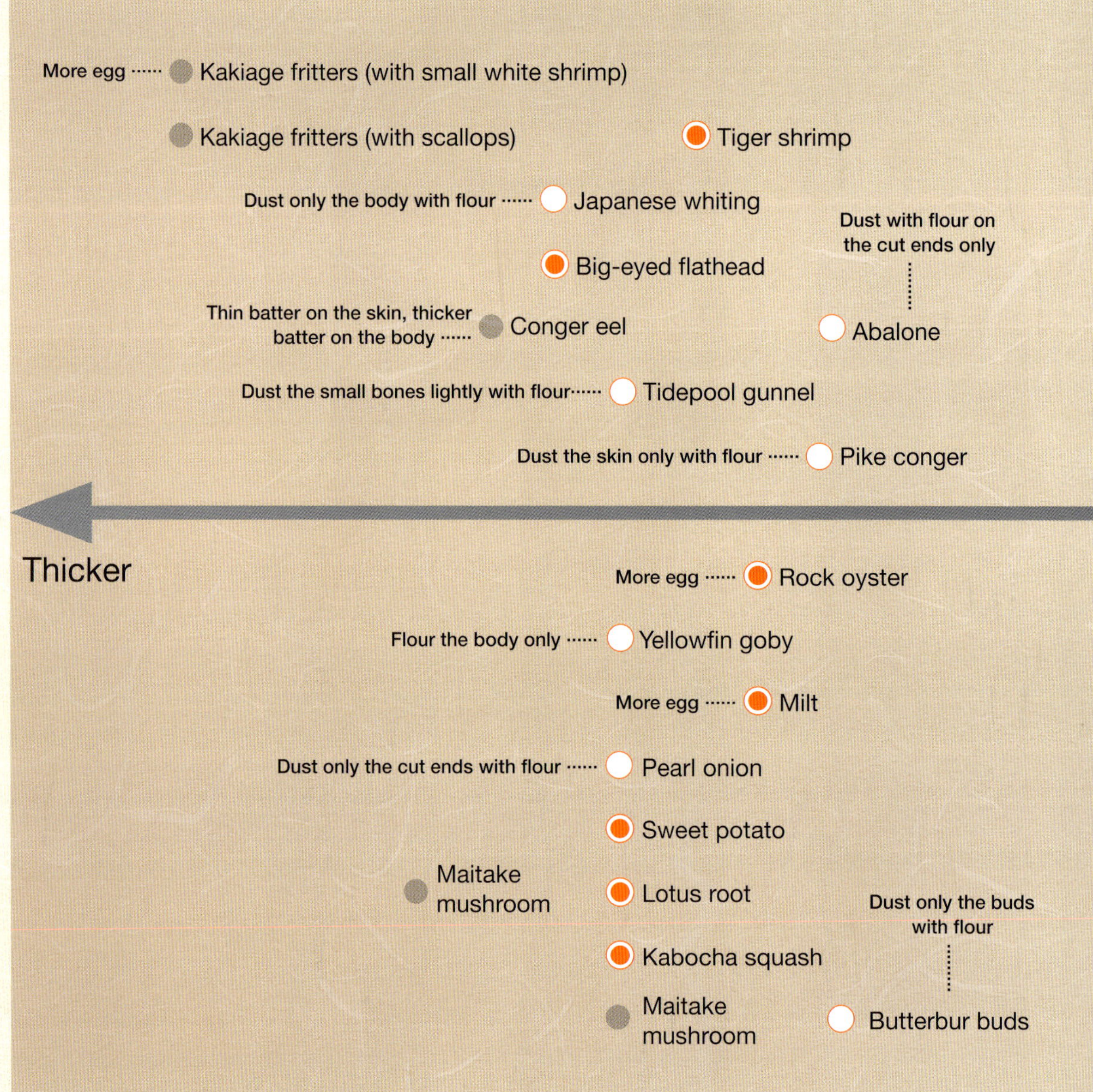

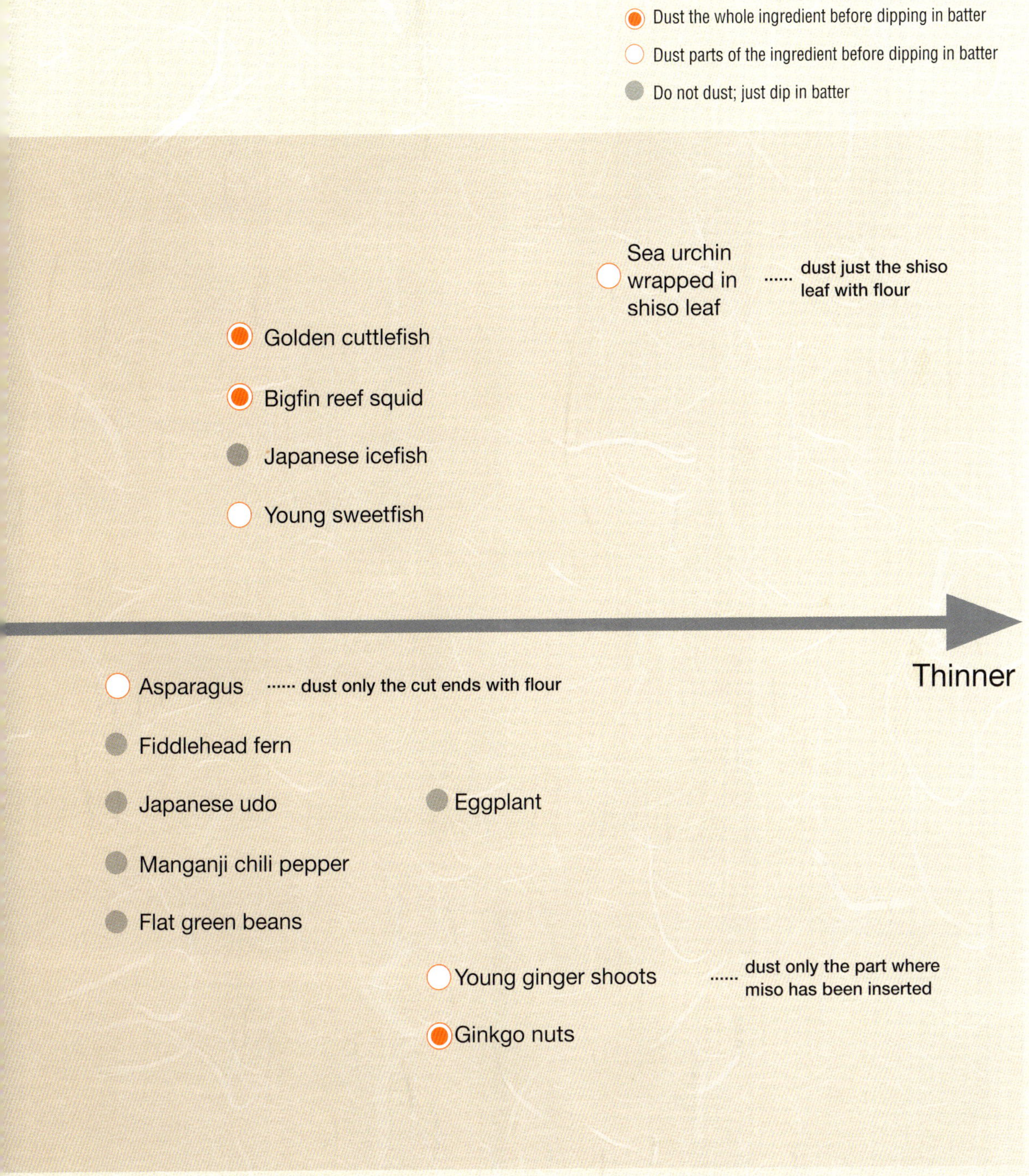

- ● Dust the whole ingredient before dipping in batter
- ○ Dust parts of the ingredient before dipping in batter
- ● Do not dust; just dip in batter

Sea urchin wrapped in shiso leaf ...... dust just the shiso leaf with flour

Golden cuttlefish

Bigfin reef squid

Japanese icefish

Young sweetfish

Thinner

Asparagus ...... dust only the cut ends with flour

Fiddlehead fern

Japanese udo

Eggplant

Manganji chili pepper

Flat green beans

Young ginger shoots ...... dust only the part where miso has been inserted

Ginkgo nuts

How to Handle Batter

The batter at Tempura Nakagawa is adjusted in one large bowl. The thickness of the batter varies according to the ingredient, so different areas of different densities of batter can be created within a single bowl. Over time, the density of the batter will change, so adjust it by moving the konabashi flour-mixing chopsticks (see page 35) around.

Key Point

The chopsticks should float in the batter

Float the chopsticks halfway into the bowl, and then let them swim in the batter without exerting too much pressure.

Key Point

Adjust batter concentration in the bowl

The consistency of the batter is varied within a single bowl. The center serves as the base, with the back portion made thicker and the left side thinner. The batter also varies by depth—thicker in the upper half and thinner in the lower half. By adjusting these areas, the ingredient can be coated with the ideal consistency of batter just before frying.

When you add cake flour to a mixture of egg and water and stir, then add more cake flour and stir again, a thicker batter forms on the surface.

Tilt the bowl to increase the surface area, making it easier to see the condition of the batter.

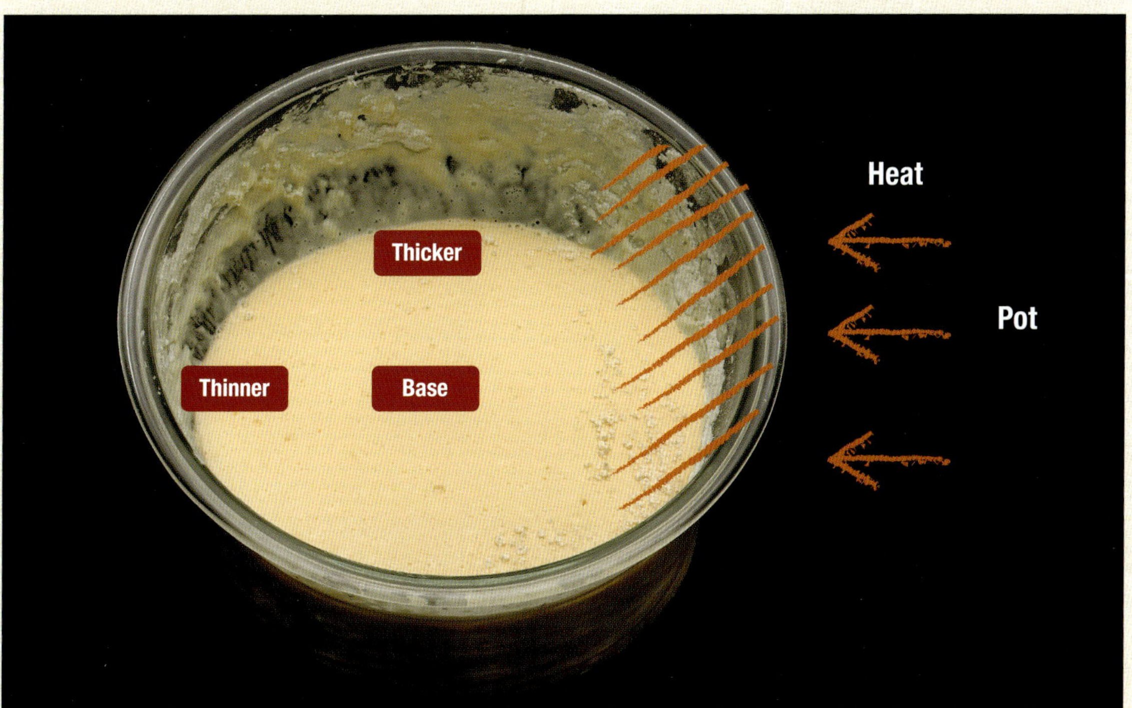

Since the battered ingredients are placed in the oil immediately after coating, the bowl is kept near the deep-frying pot. As a result, even if the bowl is ceramic with low heat conductivity, the side facing the pot gets warmer due to the heat (see illustration above). When the temperature rises, gluten begins to form in the batter, so the thicker batter on that side is balanced out by gently mixing it with the thinner batter on the cooler side using konabashi flour-mixing chopsticks.

CHAPTER 5

THE FRYING OIL

"Flavor and aroma come alive when ingredients are fried in hot oil."

—Chef Takashi Nakagawa

揚げ油

Frying Oil

Tempura wouldn't exist without the oil it's fried in. While plant-based oils are generally used, their flavor varies widely depending on the source and how they're produced – and those differences can have a significant effect on the final result.

Frying Oil
(*age abura*)

What makes deep-frying possible is that oil can be heated to high temperatures—around 390°F (200°C). Water by contrast only reaches 212°F (100°C), which results in boiling, not frying. Frying batter at 212°F or higher evaporates its moisture and replaces it with oil, resulting in crispy tempura.

The oil used for tempura is vegetable oil. Tempura specialty restaurants, especially those that claim to be Edomae style, choose rich sesame oil. However, since sesame oil on its own can be overpowering, many chefs blend it with neutral-tasting oils like cottonseed oil or light vegetable oils to create a more balanced flavor.

Sesame oil itself comes in many varieties, with differences in color, flavor, and aroma depending on how the sesame seeds are roasted and processed (page 96).

Neutral vegetable oils, often made from cottonseed, canola, corn, or sesame, are refined to have a clean, mild flavor and a smooth texture. These oils are designed not to compete with the taste of the food, making them ideal for delicate dishes like tempura.

At Tempura Nakagawa, the oil blend includes refined cottonseed oil (from Okamura Oil Co.) and light sesame oil (Shiroguchi, from Kuki Sangyo). Cottonseed oil is prized for its clean flavor and high smoke point, making it especially well-suited for deep-frying.

When selecting oil, it's important to consider not only the flavor and aroma but also how the oil performs under prolonged heat—how quickly it breaks down, how much is absorbed by the food, and how often it needs to be replaced.

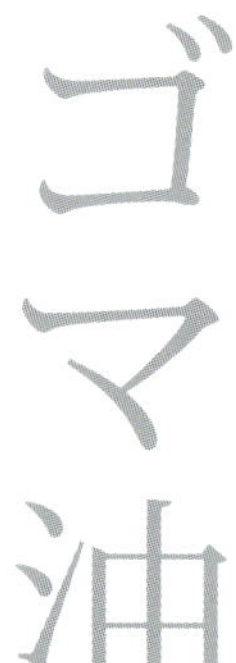

Sesame Oil

Among the many varieties of oil in which tempura can be fried, sesame oil is especially favored at specialty restaurants that offer Edomae-style tempura. Sesame oil is valued for its richness and flavor, but there are several different types. It is broadly divided into roasted sesame oil and refined sesame oil.

Sesame Oil
(*goma abura*)

Comparing tempura in the Tokyo and Osaka regions, it is said that the characteristic of Tokyo tempura is the use of sesame oil for frying. In fact, many tempura specialty restaurants claiming to be Edomae style use sesame oil.

Sesame oil can be broadly divided into two main types. One type is roasted sesame oil, known for its amber color and rich, aromatic fragrance. It is made by roasting the sesame seeds, pressing them for oil, and then filtering. The other type is refined sesame oil, made by pressing raw, unroasted sesame seeds and refining the resulting oil. This type is also known as light sesame oil.

Roasted sesame oil is sold in Japan labeled as *junsei* sesame oil or *koguchi* sesame oil. It is made by roasting sesame seeds and extracting the oil using a pressing method. The resulting oil has a toasty aroma and deep color. Impurities such as sesame seed skins are removed through repeated settling and filtration. The roasting temperature and time can be adjusted to create variations in aroma and color.

Refined sesame oil is sold in Japan labeled as *taihaku* sesame oil or *junpaku* sesame oil. It is produced by pressing raw, unroasted sesame seeds and then refining the oil.

Tempura restaurants may use roasted sesame oil only or a mixture of roasted and refined oils, depending on the flavor and finish they wish to achieve.

Manufacturing Process for Roasted Sesame Oil

Selecting the raw materials
↓
Roasting
↓
Cooling
↓
Steam cooking
↓
Pressing (oil extraction)
↓
Primary filtration
↓
Settling (aging)
↓
Final filtration

Sesame seeds are roasted and refined like other seed oils. Mild in flavor.

Sesame seeds are roasted and filtered before production. Dark amber color and unique sesame oil aroma. Strong antioxidant properties.

Varieties of Frying Oil

Tempura is typically fried in oils made from plant-based ingredients. From widely available household options to professional-grade oils, there is a wide variety depending on the source and production method. The oils shown here represent just a small selection. Color may vary by product.

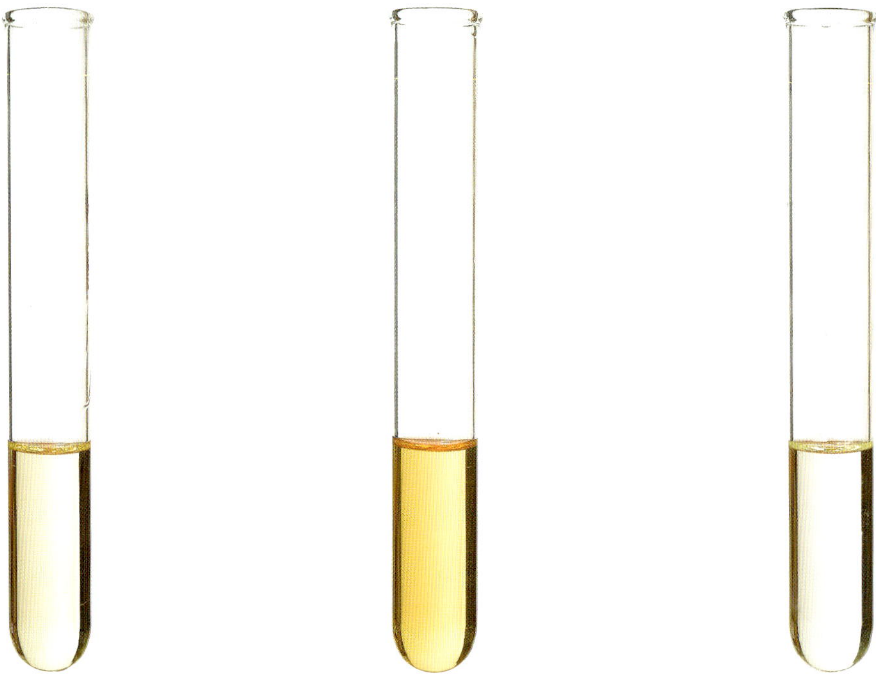

Canola Oil

Canola oil is made from the seeds of the rapeseed plant. This variety is free of erucic acid, a fatty acid that can be a health hazard. The oil content of the seeds is 30–40 percent. Canola oil is primarily composed of oleic acid, and newer varieties have been bred to further increase oleic acid content and reduce alpha-linolenic acid, which is more prone to oxidation.

Cottonseed Oil

Cotton seeds contain about 20 percent oil, which is high in linoleic acid. The oil is popular for deep-frying and canning because of its stable flavor, rich and refined umami taste, and mild aroma when heated. It is also used as a non-stick coating during the production of handmade somen noodles.

Refined Vegetable Oil

A neutral, versatile oil, called "salad oil" in Japan, originally developed to be mild enough for use in salads. Common sources include canola (rapeseed), cottonseed, soybean, sesame, corn, safflower and rice. Many refined vegetable oils are blends of two or more of these oils.

* What is shown here is only a small portion of what is available. Colors vary from product to product.

Soybean Oil

Soybeans contain about 20 percent oil, which is high in linoleic acid. While soybean oil once led global production, it has recently been surpassed by palm oil. Thanks to its rich flavor and low cost, it is widely used in cooking and is often blended with canola oil to produce refined vegetable oil.

Dark-roasted Sesame Oil

This oil has a distinctive flavor from deep roasting. Sesame seeds contain about 50 percent oil, as well as natural antioxidants (see page 99). The browning compounds formed during roasting prevent the oil from spoiling quickly. The roasting process creates a range of colors and flavor intensities, depending on the roasting time and temperature.

Safflower Oil

Safflower seeds contain about 40 percent oil. Safflower oil is regarded as a premium oil, and comes in two main varieties—one high in linoleic acid and the other high in oleic acid (see page 98). The high-oleic type is more resistant to oxidation, making it suitable for cooking at high temperatures. It has a light, neutral flavor.

The Science of Oil

Oil is composed of glycerin (also known as glycerol) bound to three fatty acids. Fatty acids are composed of three types of atoms: carbon (C), hydrogen (H) and oxygen (O); the carbon atoms are connected in a chain with a group of atoms called a carboxyl group (-COOH) at one end. There are various types of fatty acids, differing in the number of carbon atoms they contain and how those carbon atoms are bonded together.

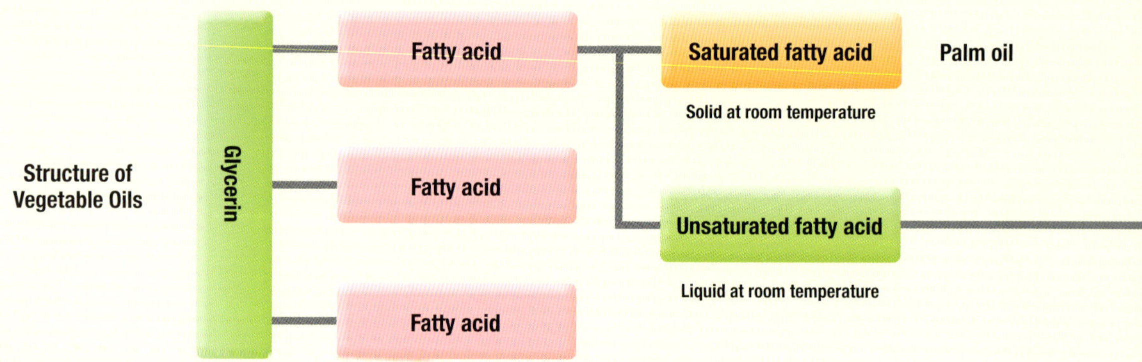

Each atom of a fatty acid has a "hand" that can bond to other atoms. The number of hands is different for each atom, with carbon atoms having four hands. Fatty acids are divided into two types: saturated and unsaturated. "Saturated" means all of a carbon atom's hands are already holding onto something—making the structure stable. "Unsaturated" means one or more hands are left unpaired, making the molecule less stable. Saturated fatty acids are found in solid fats such as beef tallow, pork fat (lard), and palm oil. Unsaturated fatty acids, on the other hand, are unstable fatty acids with double bonds, in which the carbons are connected to each other by two hands instead of one. These less stable fats are common in vegetable oils. A double bond is indicated by the equation (C = C).

Unsaturated fatty acids are further classified into monounsaturated and polyunsaturated fatty acids. Monounsaturated fatty acids have one double bond; a typical example is oleic acid. Polyunsaturated fatty acids have two or more double bonds and include linoleic acid and alpha-linolenic acid.

Oils high in oleic acid are olive oil, canola oil, high oleic sunflower oil and safflower oil; oils high in linoleic acid are soybean oil, cottonseed oil, corn oil, high linoleic sunflower oil, safflower oil and sesame oil. Oils high in alpha-linolenic acid include linseed or flaxseed oil.

In general, the more double bonds an oil contains, the lower its melting point (the temperature at which a solid turns into a liquid). For example, soybean oil, which is high in linoleic acid with two double bonds, does not solidify in the refrigerator. In contrast, olive oil, which is rich in oleic acid with only one double bond, may solidify—this difference is due to the number of double bonds.

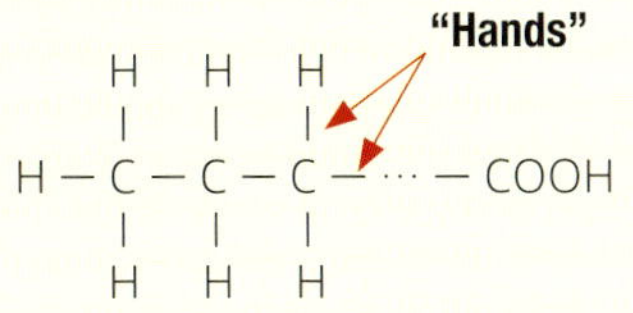

"Hands"

H — C — C — C — ··· — COOH (each C bonded to H above and below)

Saturated fatty acids (no double bonds)

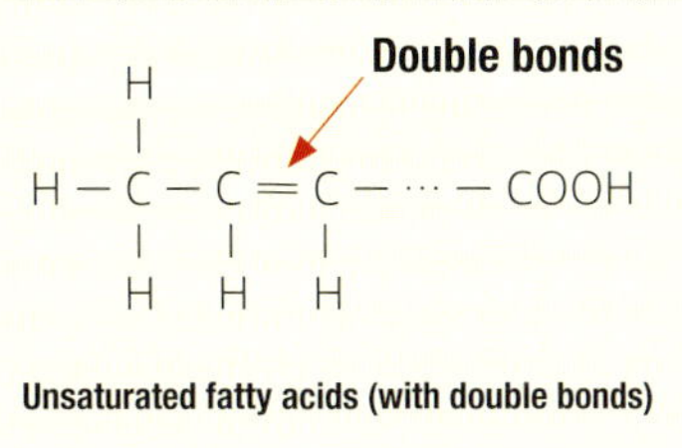

Unsaturated fatty acids (with double bonds)

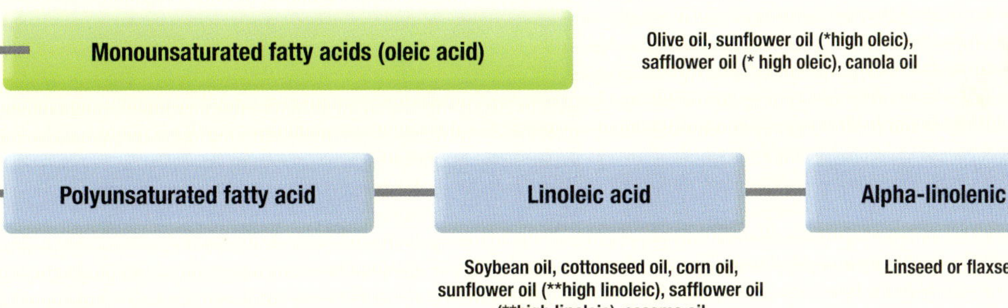

Olive oil, sunflower oil (*high oleic), safflower oil (* high oleic), canola oil

Soybean oil, cottonseed oil, corn oil, sunflower oil (**high linoleic), safflower oil (**high linoleic), sesame oil

Linseed or flaxseed oil

* High oleic = high in oleic acid

** High linoleic = high in linoleic acid

Antioxidant Effects of Roasted Sesame Oil

Although roasted sesame oil is low in vitamin E, a well-known antioxidant, it contains sesamolin, a sesame lignan with strong antioxidant effects. Sesamolin is found in sesame seeds. When sesamolin is roasted or otherwise heated to high temperatures, it is broken down into sesamol, a component with even stronger antioxidant properties that reduces oil oxidation. Sesame lignans such as sesamol, when combined with vitamin E, have a synergistic effect on antioxidant activity and are very effective in reducing oil oxidation.

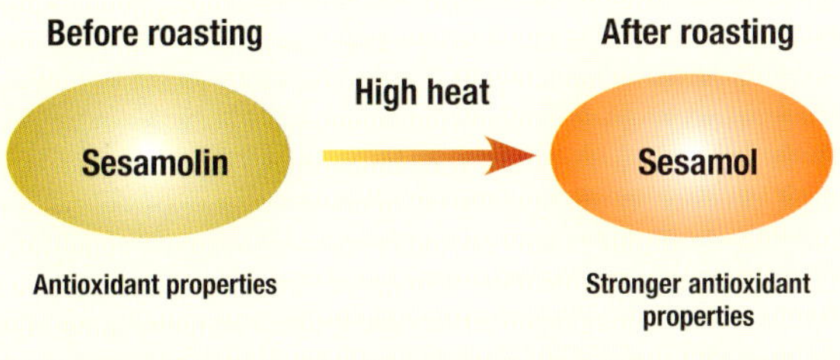

Oil Flavors

Oil's flavor depends on the raw material used, and that flavor is intensified by heating. The flavor of heated oil depends on the type and trace amounts of fatty acids originally contained in the oil. Among fatty acids, unsaturated fatty acids with double bonds are easily oxidized, and the higher the number of double bonds, the faster the oxidation rate. The oxidation of fatty acids contributes to both pleasant aromas associated with fried foods, and the distinct off-smells that come from oil degradation during cooking.

Types of fatty acids abundant in each oil

Fatty acid composition (%)		Saturated fatty acids	Monounsaturated fatty acids	Polyunsaturated fatty acids		Base ingredient	Flavor / Characteristics
Number of double bonds		0	1	2	3		
Main fatty acids		—	Oleic acid	Linoleic acid	alpha-linolenic		
Soybean oil		16	25	52	7	Soybeans	Distinctive umami and richness
Rapeseed oil	—	8	16	12	9	Rapeseed plant seeds	Light, mild flavor
	Canola oil	8	64	19	9	Improved rapeseed seeds	
Cottonseed oil		23	19	57	1	Cotton plant seeds	Unique, elegant flavor, less oily smell (high quality oil)
Corn oil		14	31	54	1	Corn germ	Unique nutty flavor
Sunflower oil	high linoleic	11	31	58	0	Sunflower seeds	Light flavor, no distinctive characteristics
	high oleic	9	84	7	0		
Safflower oil	high linoleic	10	17	73	0	Safflower seeds	
	high oleic	8	78	14	0		
Sesame oil		16	40	44	0	Sesame seeds	**Roasted sesame oil:** unique color and aroma **Cold-pressed sesame oil:** rich in umami and sweetness
Virgin olive oil		14	75	7	1	Olive	Unique flavor and aroma

The main fatty acids found in vegetable oils are oleic acid, linoleic acid and alpha-linolenic acid. Oleic acid, with one double bond, is less susceptible to oxidation than linoleic acid and alpha-linolenic acid, which have two or more double bonds, and it produces less flavor when heated. Linoleic acid, when heated produces a so-called tempura smell, which gives fried foods a pleasant flavor, but it also produces the off-smell typical of degraded oil. Alpha-linolenic acid, when heated, gives off a heavy, unpleasant odor that can cause queasiness.

The proportion of fatty acids in oil varies with the type of oil, and the flavor of each oil depends on that proportion. Soybean oil and canola oil produce the characteristic aroma of fried foods when heated, but because they

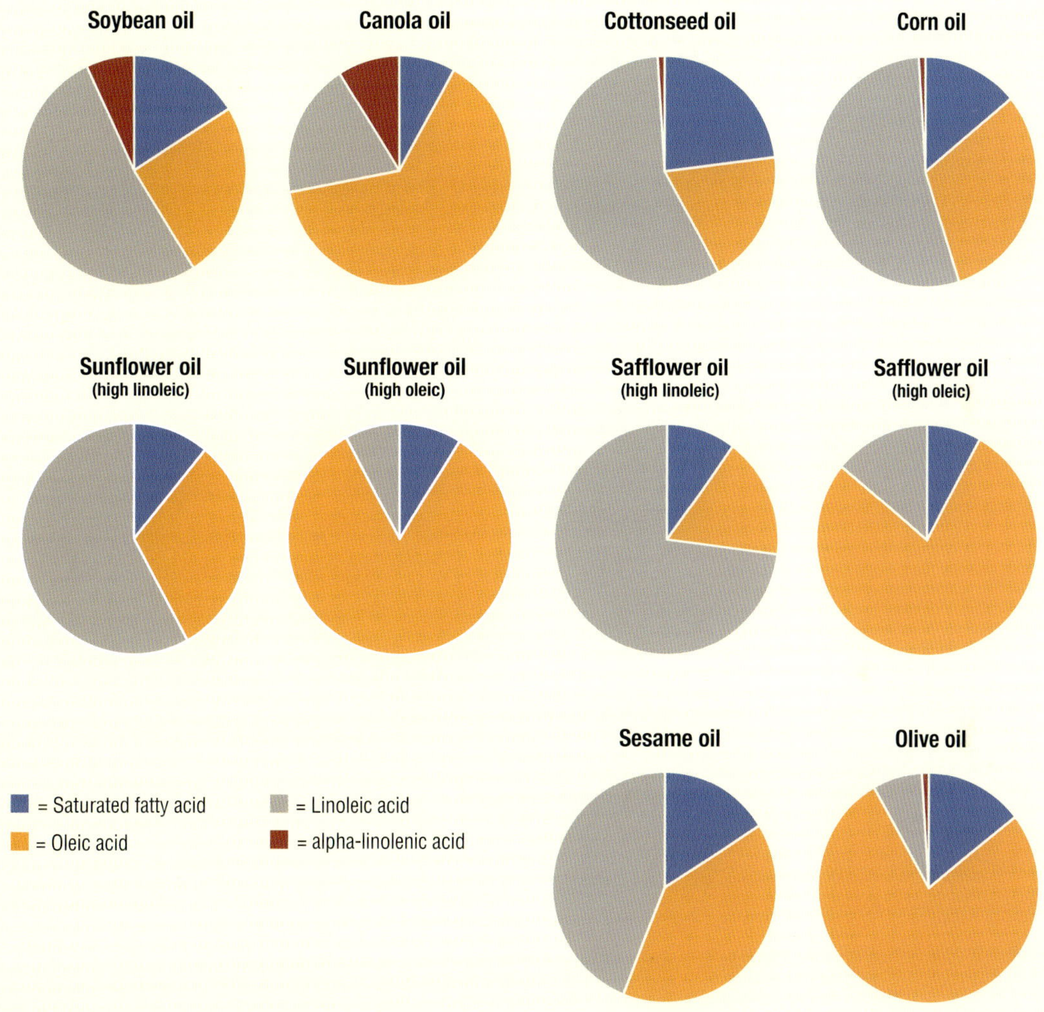

contain a high amount of alpha-linolenic acid, they also develop the distinctive off-smell of heated oil. In contrast, sunflower oil and safflower oil, which contain very little alpha-linolenic acid, have a mild and neutral flavor with no strong aftertaste. Corn oil, sesame oil and olive oil, which also contain little alpha-linolenic acid, tend to exhibit the distinctive flavors of their original ingredients more strongly. Of the three unsaturated fatty acids commonly found in vegetable oils, oleic acid is the most resistant to oxidation. Linoleic acid follows, and alpha-linolenic acid is the most prone to oxidation. For high-heat cooking methods like tempura, oils high in oleic acid are best. Sesame oil has a well-balanced composition of oleic and linoleic acids and also possesses antioxidant properties—one of the reasons it is often used as oil for tempura.

Preparation

Tentsuyu Dipping Sauce for Tempura

Tentsuyu is a tempura dipping sauce that does not detract from the flavor of the ingredients, but adds a new dimension to the flavor of the tempura. The basic dashi stock for tentsuyu is made from kombu seaweed, katsuobushi bonito flakes, and dried shiitake mushrooms, with soy sauce and mirin to taste.

How to Make Tentsuyu

MAKES 7½ QUARTS (7 L)

4½ quarts (4.4 L) dashi stock (see below)
6¼ cups (1.5 L) soy sauce
4¼ cups (1.1 L) mirin

Combine all the ingredients, bring to a boil, and let cool.

How to Make Dashi Stock

MAKES 10½ QUARTS (10 L)

2½ oz (70 g) kombu seaweed (Rishiri variety)
10½ quarts (10 L) water
2 oz (60 g) dried shiitake mushrooms
10 oz (300 g) katsuobushi bonito flakes

1. Soak the kombu in the water overnight. Add the shiitake and heat over medium heat.
2. Take out the kombu just before the liquid comes to a boil. Just before you add the bonito flakes, remove the shiitake.
3. Add the bonito flakes, push the flakes to the bottom of the pot with chopsticks, turn off the heat, and strain.

Preparation

Daikon Oroshi

Daikon oroshi (grated daikon radish) is a refreshing accompaniment to tempura. It can be added to the tentsuyu sauce or eaten as is between bites of tempura — it plays the perfect supporting role. It also offers nutritional benefits: the spiciness of daikon stimulates gastric juice secretion and aids digestion, and it contains enzymes that support the function of the stomach and intestines.

The Paper Liner

Tempura is served on a paper liner called a shikigami, whose use originates with food offerings made to Shinto gods. The way the shikigami is folded differs depending on the occasion — whether it's a joyful celebration or a time of mourning, such as a funeral. The paper has a smooth side and a rough side; the smooth side is considered the front.

How to Fold the Paper Liner

The way to fold the paper is different for celebrations and occasions of mourning. The top left corner points up for celebrations, and the top right corner points up for mourning.

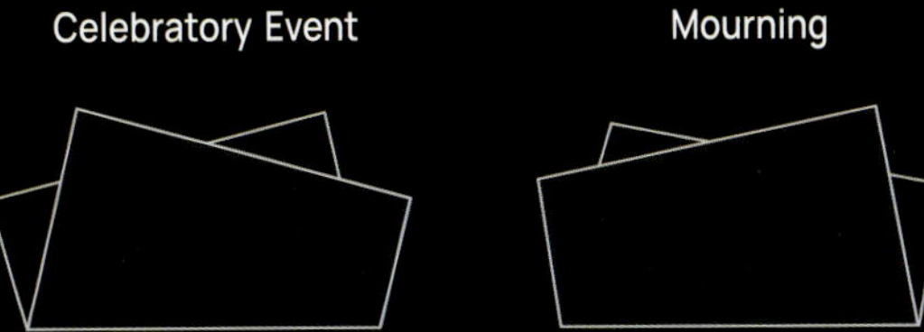

CHAPTER 6

DEEP-FRYING TECHNIQUES

"Aim for a moist, delicate interior and a crispy coating."

—Chef Takashi Nakagawa

揚げる

Deep-frying

As tempura cooks, in high-temperature oil, it changes state by the second, requiring constant and immediate attention. The process is simple – coating a carefully prepared ingredient in batter and placing it in the oil – but the chef must observe how the batter disperses, the state of the bubbles, the movement of the oil, and even the weight felt through the frying chopsticks (see page 36). By closely reading these changes in both the ingredient and the oil, the tempura can be removed at precisely the right moment.

Deep-frying (*ageru*)

Tempura can be fried in two main ways: lightly or thoroughly. Japanese people always say tempura in the Osaka region is lightly fried in clear oil and served with salt, while tempura in the Tokyo region is fried in roasted sesame oil and served with tentsuyu sauce. But nowadays lightly fried tempura is often seen in both the Tokyo and Osaka regions. The tempura at Tempura Nakagawa follows the Tokyo-style tradition of deep-frying. This is the belief of Chef Takashi Nakagawa, who says, "by frying the ingredients thoroughly, the heat fully penetrates them—only then can their true flavor and aroma be brought out."

Chef Nakagawa blends roasted sesame oil with cottonseed oil and deep-fries the tempura at 390°F (200°C), which is higher than the generally accepted frying temperature of 355°F (180°C).

Tempura is often described as a cooking method that "steams" the ingredient inside its batter coating by frying at high heat. But Chef Nakagawa says it's not just about steaming—he also thinks of it as "baking the batter" in the oil. By steaming the ingredient inside the coating and browning the outside as if baking it, he brings out a flavor and aroma that only tempura can deliver.

Temperature Changes in the Deep-frying Oil at Tempura Nakagawa

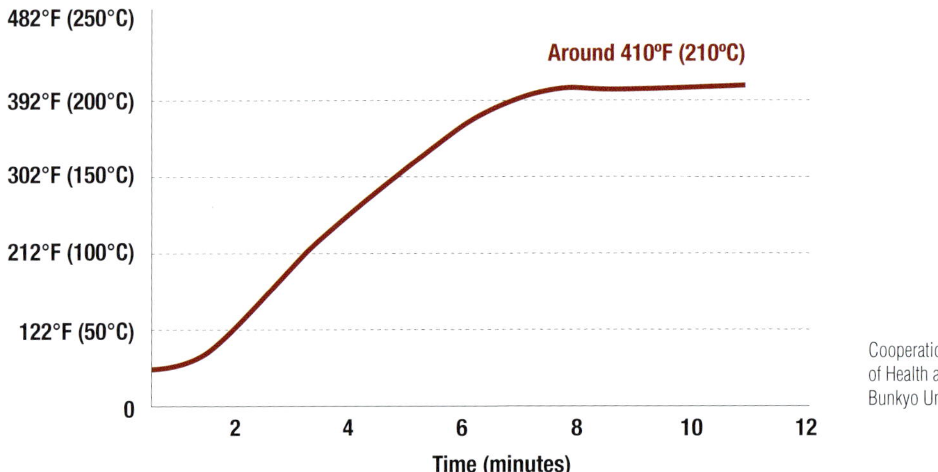

Cooperation: Faculty of Health and Nutrition, Bunkyo University

These are the temperature changes of oil measured in a room with a ambient temperature of 78°F (25.5°C). The heat source used was a commercial gas burner powered by natural gas, with a gas output of 11.6 kW – stronger than typical home stovetops. About 7 minutes after ignition, the temperature rose to around 410°F (210°C). The heat is adjusted to fry the ingredients at around 390–410°F (200–210°C).

1

Fill about 70 percent of the pot with oil, and heat on a gas stove or induction cooktop. When warm, stir with chopsticks to eliminate the temperature difference between the top and the bottom.

2

Check the temperature by dropping in a little batter. It depends somewhat on the consistency of the batter, but if it scatters across the surface of the oil as shown in the photo, that's a good indication the temperature is around 390°F (200°C).

3

Remove the tempura batter bits using a net skimmer. Stir the oil to create a circulating flow, then place the strainer so that it blocks the flow — the batter bits will naturally collect on the strainer.

The Science of Deep-frying

Deep-frying is the phenomenon of exchanging water and oil

During the tempura frying process, a phenomenon known as the "water–oil exchange" occurs: as the moisture in the batter evaporates, oil fills the spaces left behind. When the moisture in the batter is thoroughly removed and oil properly takes its place, the result is a crisp, light texture. But if the moisture isn't fully driven out and oil doesn't penetrate the batter, the texture becomes soggy and heavy.

The reason a batter that hasn't undergone a full water–oil exchange feels greasy and heavy is because the oil clings to the surface of the batter and comes into direct contact with the membranes in your mouth. When the exchange is successful and oil is fully absorbed into the batter, the slightly dried, crisp texture is perceived as "lightness."

The ingredient wrapped in the batter is essentially being steamed inside the coating. Because of this, vegetables retain and intensify their natural sweetness and aroma, while seafood preserves its inherent umami—allowing the full character of the ingredient to shine through.

Changes in Moisture and Oil Content in Batter

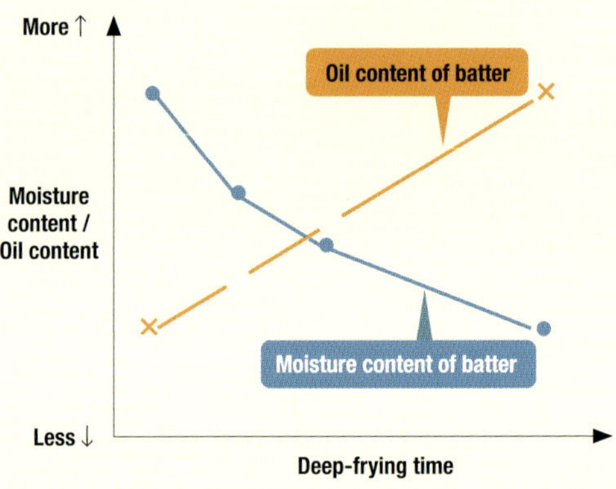

As frying time increases, the moisture in the batter gradually decreases, while the amount of oil absorbed into the batter increases.

The "Replacement Phenomenon" of Water and Oil in the Batter

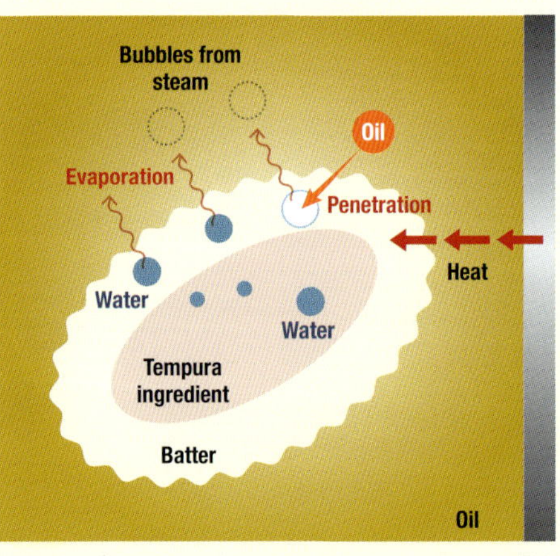

Heat transfer during the deep-frying process

With tempura, the batter and the ingredient have different compositions and properties, yet both must reach their ideal state at the same temperature and in the same cooking time. It is therefore essential to understand how heat is transferred to both the batter and the ingredient during frying.

During frying, heat is transferred via the oil, moving from the batter to the ingredient. At the start of frying, the heat from the oil raises the temperature of the batter. Once the batter reaches 212°F (100°C), most of the heat is used to evaporate its moisture. At this stage, the temperature of the ingredient inside barely increases. As the moisture in the batter begins to evaporate, heat starts to transfer from the batter to the ingredient, and its internal temperature gradually rises.

The vapor that rapidly evaporates from the batter causes the oil to foam vigorously.

The moisture that has moved from the ingredients to the batter is emitted as small bubbles of vapor.

Temperature Changes in Frying Oil and Ingredients

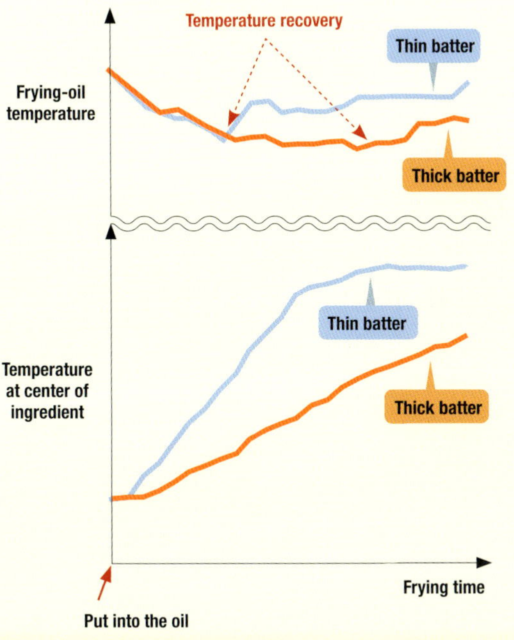

Oil heats up and cools down easily, rising and falling in temperature twice as fast as water. When ingredients are added to the frying oil, the oil temperature drops rapidly. After that, the temperature of the oil is restored as heat continues to transfer from the heat source, but since part of that heat is used to evaporate moisture from the batter, the recovery is slow.

The speed at which the oil temperature recovers after adding the ingredient is also affected by the thickness of the batter: thinner batter allows the temperature to rebound more quickly, because thinner batter contains less moisture, so less heat is consumed in the evaporation process.

What is oil degradation?

When tempura is fried repeatedly in the same oil, the oil which starts out light and silky becomes viscous and thick, a condition called "oil degradation."

As oil degrades, its viscosity increases, and other changes occur as well: discoloration, unpleasant odors, smoke, and a type of persistent bubbling known as *kani-awa*, meaning "crab foam." Kani-awa refers to the fine bubbles that spread and swell across the surface of the oil when an ingredient is added, and that linger for some time even after the tempura is removed. Using degraded oil not only gives the tempura a poor color and unpleasant smell, but also disrupts the smooth exchange of moisture and oil, resulting in a greasy, heavy coating.

The main cause of oil degradation is a chemical reaction called oxidation, in which oxygen in the air reacts with the fatty acids in the oil. This causes discoloration, off-odors, and other signs of deterioration. As oxidation progresses, a reaction called polymerization occurs, where oil molecules bond together to form long-chain compounds. These high-molecular-weight compounds increase the oil's viscosity and also cause crab foam to form. Both oxidation and polymerization accelerate significantly at high temperatures—raising the temperature by just 50°F (10°C) is said to speed up these reactions by about three to five times. When moisture is present in the oil, this also promotes degradation. Since tempura is typically fried at high temperatures using batter and ingredients with high moisture content, it creates ideal conditions for oil to break down quickly.

While degraded oil cannot be restored, there is a way to slow the degradation process: adding fresh oil. This means topping off the oil with a small amount of fresh oil each time you fry. By repeatedly diluting the degraded oil with fresh oil, the overall rate of deterioration is reduced compared to using the same batch of oil continuously.

Unused oil (left), and oil after frying (right). After frying, the oil is viscous and colored. Some of the coloration comes from the tempura batter and some from the oxidation and polymerization reactions in the oil.

The Smoke Point of Oil

Type	Smoke point		Antioxidant ingredients	
	Refined	Unrefined	Vitamin E (mg/per 100 ml oil)	Other
Soybean oil	446–495°F (230–257°C)	320°F (160°C)	10	–
Rapeseed oil / Canola oil	399–450°F (204–232°C)	225°F (107°C)	15	–
Cottonseed oil	421–451°F (216–233°C)	–	28	–
Corn oil	450°F (232°C)	320°F (160°C)	17	–
Sunflower oil	450–511°F (232–266°C)	225°F (107°C)	39	–
Safflower oil	450–511°F (232–266°C)	225°F (107°C)	27	–
Sesame oil	450°F (232°C)	329–351°F (165–177°C)	0	Sesame lignans
Virgin olive oil	–	320–374°F (160–190°C)	7	Oleuropein Beta-carotene

The smoke point of oil (the temperature at which oil begins to smoke when heated) varies depending on the type of oil and how it has been refined. Unrefined oils tend to have low smoke points, typically around 225°F to 350°F (107°C to 177°C). Refining removes impurities and other non-oil substances, raising the smoke point of refined oils to around 400°F to 510°F (204°C to 266°C). However, even the smoke point of refined oils decreases over time. As it is used for frying, it undergoes oxidation and breakdown, increasing the amount of non-oil substances. The longer the oil is used and the higher the frying temperature, the more these substances accumulate.

As non-oil components increase, the oil may become sticky, tinted, or develop crab foam. The flavor and texture of food fried in this oil will deteriorate. It is important to control the oxidation of the oil to minimize oil degradation.

Oils contain natural antioxidants—substances that suppress oxidation—such as vitamin E and sesame lignans. These antioxidants come from the oil's source ingredients, so the type and amount present will vary depending on the raw material. While their antioxidant strength may differ, all of them help slow oxidation during cooking.

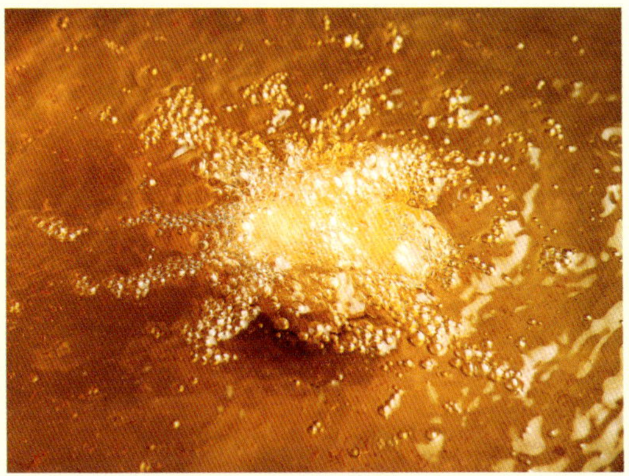

The Science of Frying Seafood

When seafood flesh (muscle) is heated, it first becomes more tender than when raw, but then turns firm. This change is related to the fact that the three types of proteins that make up the flesh each solidify at different temperatures when heated (see pages 62–63).

As the internal temperature of the flesh rises, the myofibrillar proteins are the first to coagulate from the heat. At this stage, the sarcoplasmic proteins—those water-soluble proteins that fill the spaces between the myofibrils—have not yet coagulated, so when bitten into, the myofibrils still move easily, making the flesh feel softer than when raw. As the temperature rises further, the sarcoplasmic proteins also coagulate, acting like glue to bind the myofibrils together. Once this happens, the myofibrils no longer move freely when chewed, and the flesh feels firmer than when raw. With even higher heat, the collagen that bundles the muscle fibers contracts rapidly, making the flesh even firmer and squeezing the juices out from the muscle fibers. The contraction temperature of collagen in fish flesh is 100–140°F (38–60°C), and tends to be lower in fish from cold waters compared to those from warm waters. In shrimp and squid, collagen contraction begins around 122°F (50°C).

In tempura, the flesh is enclosed in a batter coating, so even if the collagen contracts slightly and some juices are squeezed out of the muscle fibers, they remain within the coating, preventing the flesh from drying out. However, in seafood like shrimp and squid, which contain a large amount of collagen, the collagen can constrict the muscle fibers strongly, causing the flesh to dry out and become tough. The ideal timing to remove such items from the frying oil is when their internal temperature reaches around 122°F (50°C).

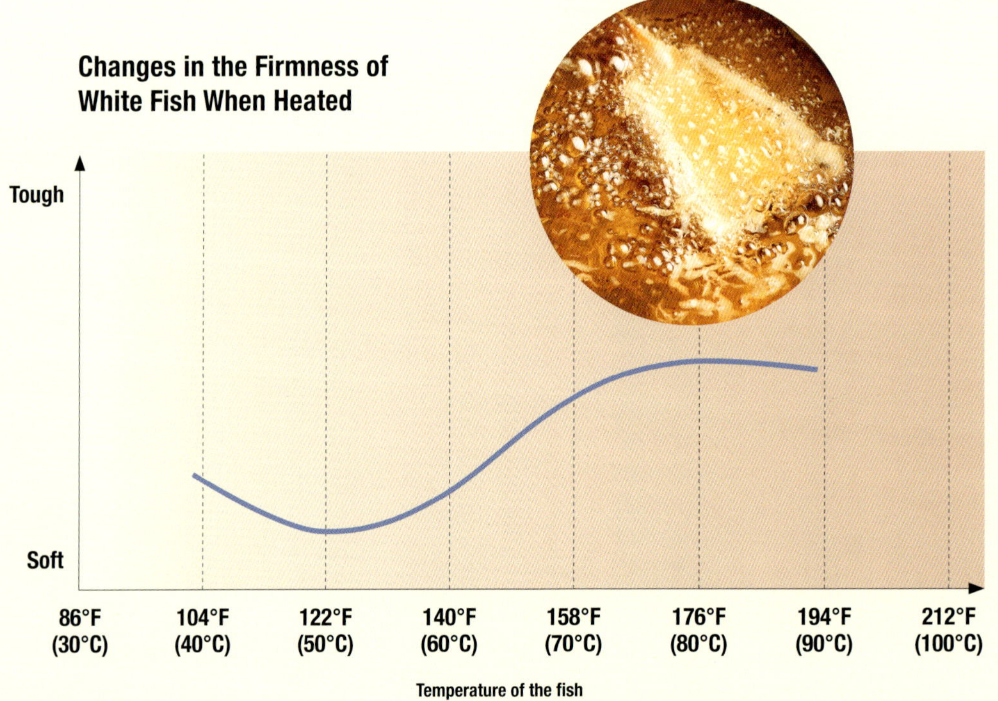

Created with data from *Sakana no kagaku* (The Science of Fish), Asakura Shoten, 1994.

Temperature Changes in Shrimp at Tempura Nakagawa

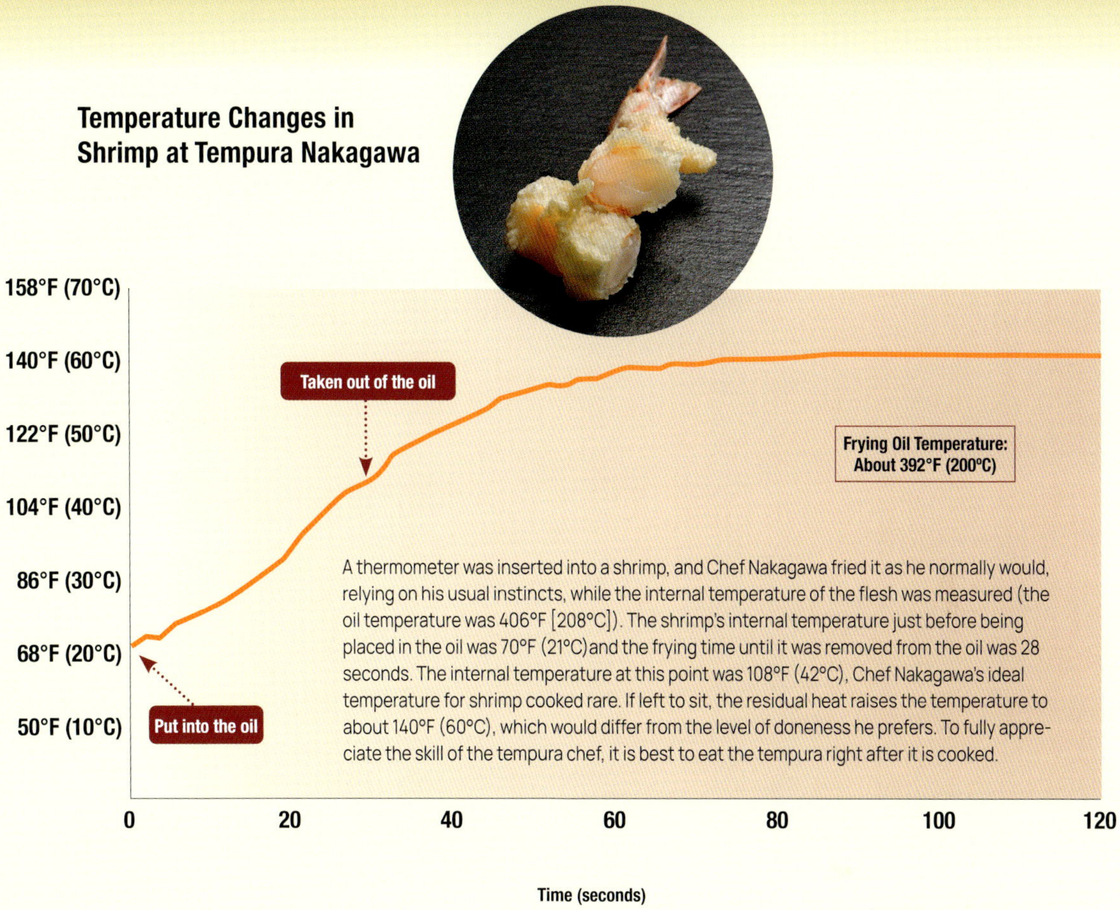

158°F (70°C)
140°F (60°C)
122°F (50°C)
104°F (40°C)
86°F (30°C)
68°F (20°C)
50°F (10°C)
Taken out of the oil
Put into the oil
Frying Oil Temperature: About 392°F (200°C)
A thermometer was inserted into a shrimp, and Chef Nakagawa fried it as he normally would, relying on his usual instincts, while the internal temperature of the flesh was measured (the oil temperature was 406°F [208°C]). The shrimp's internal temperature just before being placed in the oil was 70°F (21°C)and the frying time until it was removed from the oil was 28 seconds. The internal temperature at this point was 108°F (42°C), Chef Nakagawa's ideal temperature for shrimp cooked rare. If left to sit, the residual heat raises the temperature to about 140°F (60°C), which would differ from the level of doneness he prefers. To fully appreciate the skill of the tempura chef, it is best to eat the tempura right after it is cooked.
0
20
40
60
80
100
120
Time (seconds)

Cooperation: Faculty of Health and Nutrition, Bunkyo University
(Varies depending on room temperature, shrimp condition, and other frying parameters.)

Muscle Changes Due to Heat

Myofibrillar protein
Sarcoplasmic protein
Apply heat

When the myofibrillar proteins have coagulated from heat but the sarcoplasmic proteins have not yet solidified, the flesh offers little resistance when bitten into, making it feel more tender than when raw. Next, when the sarcoplasmic proteins also coagulate and the flesh becomes a unified mass, it offers greater resistance to the bite, making it feel firmer than when raw. If the item is removed from the oil before the collagen contracts from heat, the result is a tender and gently textured tempura.

When chewed the fibers shift
Hardens
Apply heat
Still not hardened
Everything hardens

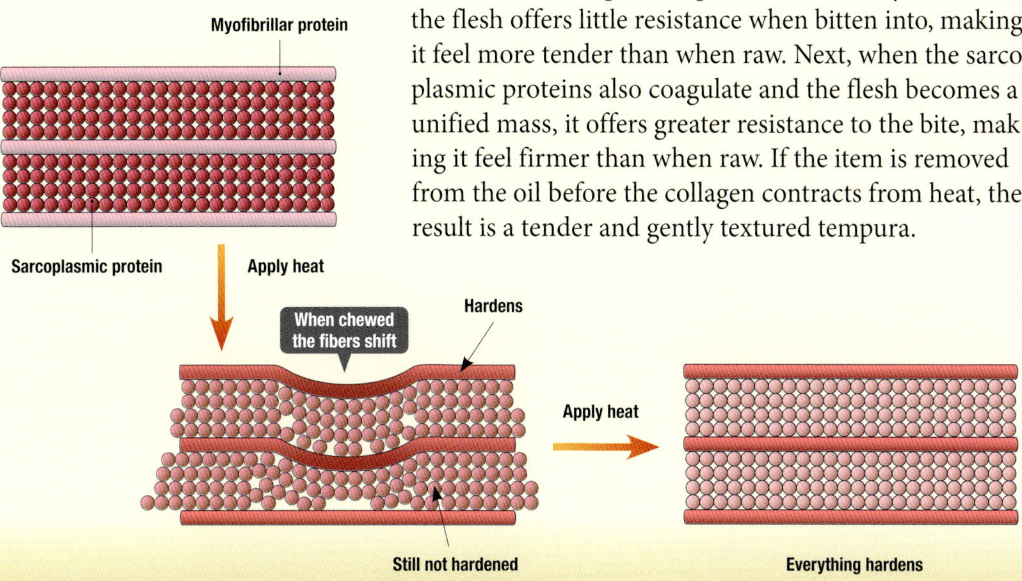

Seafood Tempura

Seafood for Edomae tempura is prepared using ingredients fresh enough to be eaten raw. Some are butterflied, others are left whole, and all are readied to be quickly coated in batter and immediately placed into hot oil. The degree of doneness is adjusted to suit each ingredient — conger eel is well-cooked, while tiger shrimp may be left slightly rare. In each case, the tempura is removed from the oil just before it is fully cooked, taking residual heat into account to finish it perfectly.

The batter is fried until crispy and the ingredient within is steamed, to bring out the best flavor.

Tiger Shrimp
(*kuruma ebi*)

Tiger Shrimp

ORDER: Decapoda **FAMILY:** Penaeidae **SCIENTIFIC NAME:** Marsupenaeus japonicus

Larger shrimp over 6 inches (15 cm) are called *kuruma ebi*, while smaller shrimp of 4–6 inches (10–15 cm) are called *saimaki*. They used to be found at depths of 150–300 feet (50–100 meters) in bays throughout Japan, but natural populations have been drastically reduced due to land reclamation and other factors.

Total length: 6½ inches (17 cm)

Tiger shrimp are the star attraction of Edomae tempura. The red color that peeks through the batter is beautiful, and the rich sweetness and springy texture are especially appealing. To maximize flavor, fry at a high temperature for a short time to achieve a medium-rare center. Just before frying, the shrimp is prepared live—its head is removed, and the shell is peeled. To ensure even coating, it's dipped into the batter once or twice, then immediately placed into the hot oil. It's fried for about 30 seconds. From the moment it's placed in the oil to the moment it's done, the entire process takes just about one minute. At the point of doneness, the core temperature of the shrimp is around 122°F (50°C). The head is fried longer than the body for a different nuttier flavor.

1 Hold the live shrimp with its body slightly bent back, and gently insert your thumb into the joint between the head and the body.

2 Remove the head and intestines at the same time, being careful not to tear the intestines.

3 Peel off the shell from the leg side.

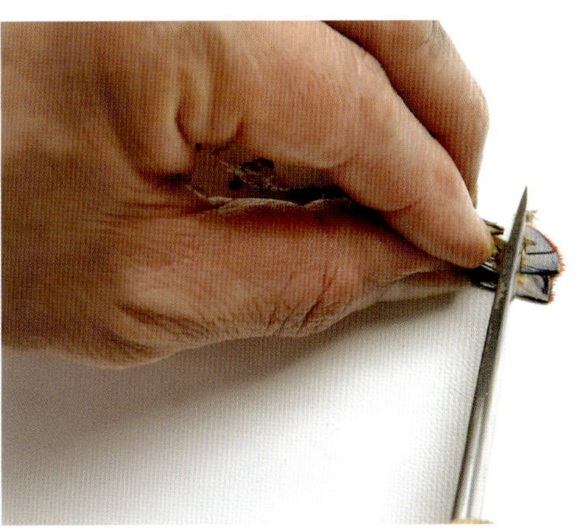

4 Press and stretch the sides of the body to prevent it from curling up.

5 Cut off the tail end as it will burst when fried.

6 Process the head. Peel off the shell, remove the eyes, and extract the head matter.

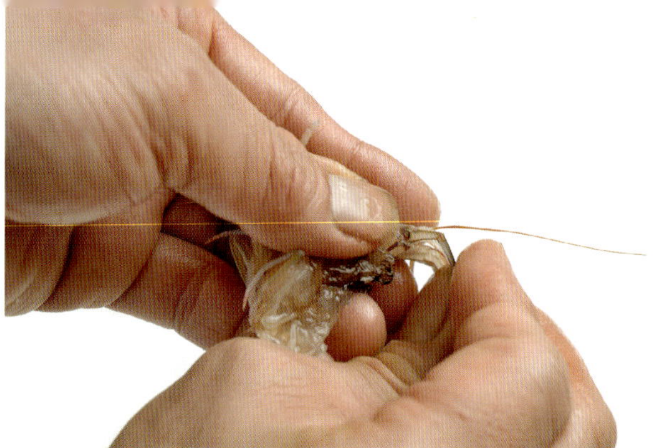

7 Break off the rostrum — the hard, pointed projection extending from the shrimp's head.

8 Dust with flour.

9 Dip into the batter once or twice to ensure an even coating.

Head and body of the peeled tiger shrimp. The head is fried until crisp, while the body is fried to a tender finish

10 Immediately put the shrimp into the oil. After about 15 seconds, depending on its condition, turn it over and fry for another 15 seconds. Remove after a total of 30 seconds.

The tiger shrimp is stretched straight and has a beautiful red color that peeks through the batter. The center is fried to a medium rare, offering a burst of sweetness and a springy texture beneath the crisp coating. Truly the star of tempura.

The head of the tiger shrimp is simply dusted with flour with no batter applied, and fried until crispy and fragrant. The small bits of meat are sweet, and you can enjoy a rich flavor and a light texture.

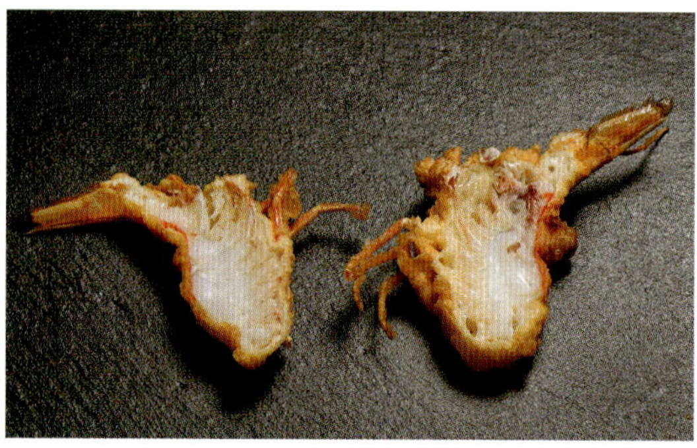

Cross-section of the shrimp head: by frying it slowly, the outside becomes crisp while the meat inside is evenly and perfectly cooked through.

TECHNIQUE FOCUS

Deep-frying Two Pieces of Tiger Shrimp Tempura Separately

A course at Tempura Nakagawa begins with tiger shrimp. Two tiger shrimp are served; the first one is fried differently from the second one. Even the most delicious food can start to feel monotonous if served the same way twice in a row, so this variation is intended to let guests experience the shrimp's flavor more deeply.

The deliciousness of shrimp lies in its plump texture and unique sweetness. The same base concept of "a half-raw state that is a little warmer than body temperature" is used for both pieces, but each is finished a little differently. To counter the "familiarity" of the taste of the first tiger shrimp, the second tiger shrimp is cooked at a higher temperature with more intense heat from the oil (see page 127) and removed from the oil a few seconds earlier than the first tiger shrimp, so that the sweetness is more pronounced.

How to Get the Right Oil Ratio

At Tempura Nakagawa the frying oil is a mixture of sesame oil and cottonseed oil. More cottonseed oil results in a lighter finish, while a higher proportion of sesame oil adds richness and aroma. The initial ratio is about 45 percent sesame oil to 55 percent cottonseed oil, and the mixture is adjusted by repeatedly adding more sesame oil or more cottonseed oil while frying different kinds of ingredients.

Fish with slimy skin such as conger eel and big-eyed flathead will have an unpleasant smell if they are not fried well enough, but when fried well that sliminess is transformed into a nutty aroma. To achieve this, more sesame oil is used. "Frying thoroughly in a sesame oil–rich blend brings out the unique flavor and aroma of the fish," says Chef Takashi Nakagawa. The same goes for vegetables, such as ginkgo nuts, asparagus and pearl onions, which can be made sweeter and more aromatic by adding more sesame oil.

These adjustments are made in real time as the tempura course is served. After frying the shrimp body first, more sesame oil is added to fry the head slowly and bring out a deeper aroma. Next comes whiting, which has a delicate flavor, so cottonseed oil is added. When the course moves to seasonal vegetables, more sesame oil is added; for squid, more cottonseed oil is added; and toward the end, for conger eel and big-eyed flathead, sesame oil is added again in larger amounts. Throughout the meal, the oil isn't just replenished—it's also reduced or skimmed to adjust the balance and maintain the right "strength" (see facing page), creating the ideal frying environment for each tempura ingredient.

Adjusting the "Strength" of the Oil

Tempura chefs talk about "strength" to describe the condition of the oil used to fry tempura. When the oil has strength, the oil is silky smooth, and when it does not have strength, the oil is viscous and thick.

Even with new oil, when the temperature is low, the oil does not yet have strength because of its viscosity. But as the temperature rises, it becomes thinner and silkier. This is the state where the oil has strength. But as frying continues, the oil becomes dirty and oxidized and its viscosity increases even at high temperatures. When this happens, the oil has no strength. This kind of assessment of the oil's condition is necessary throughout the tempura-frying process.

The graph represents how Chef Nakagawa conceptualizes oil strength during frying. Oil strength is determined by both the condition of the oil and its temperature, i.e., the level of heat applied. Oil with strong power (labeled A) reaches the target temperature quickly, while weaker oil (labeled B) takes longer to get there. That doesn't mean A is always better—depending on the ingredient, the oil may need to be intentionally brought down to a B-level strength. For example, when frying starchy items like potatoes that need to be cooked slowly, the heat is lowered to reduce the oil's strength.

If you feel the oil has lost its strength after frying, strain out some of the old oil and add new oil to increase its strength. In this way, the cook adjusts the condition and temperature of the oil to match the ingredient and reach the ideal level of "oil strength."

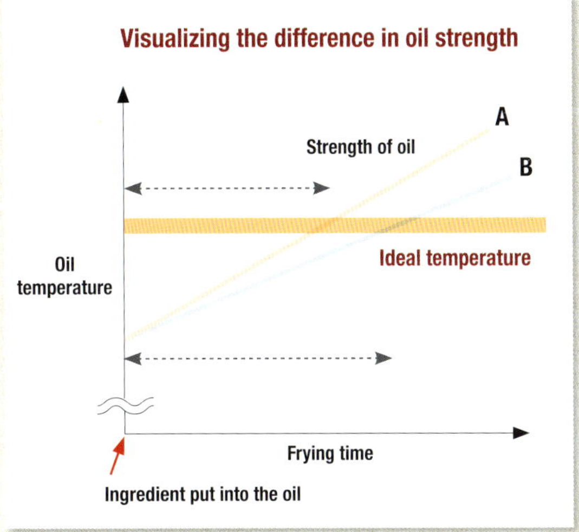

Control the Oil Temperature with Tempura Batter Bits

The tenkasu tempura batter bits that float off the tempura pieces help control the temperature during the frying process. For example, Japanese whiting takes a long time to fry, so if the temperature is even slightly too high, the batter will burn; and if the temperature is low, the batter will not fry crisply. To fine-tune the temperature, the tempura batter bits that scatter into the oil when the ingredient is added are left on the surface. These help prevent sudden spikes in oil temperature. Once the temperature has settled, the batter bits are removed, and the ingredient is fried slowly and carefully.

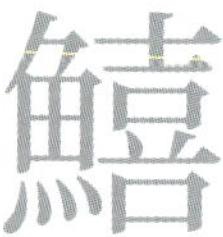

Japanese Whiting (*kisu*)

Japanese Whiting

Japanese whiting is butterflied along the back. Its flesh is extremely delicate and mild in flavor, so the key is to fry it in a way that prevents it from tasting watery. To achieve this, it must be fried gently and evenly to allow just the right amount of moisture to escape while keeping the texture tender. To balance how the heat and moisture affect the skin and the flesh, flour is dusted only on the flesh side, not on the skin. Then it's dipped in batter and placed into the oil. Because the batter tends to slide off when the fish hits the oil, it's important to slide the fillet in quickly from the head side, so the coating stays even.

How to Prepare Japanese Whiting ➡ page 42

1 Dust only the flesh with flour.

2 Dip the fish in a slightly thick batter. Lift it out with chopsticks and let the excess batter drip off.

Among white fish, Japanese whiting is considered the pinnacle of tempura. If overcooked, it feels heavy; if undercooked, it turns out watery – so it's essential to get the battering and frying just right. The goal is a crisp exterior, a moist interior, and a fluffy, tender texture that brings out the whiting's delicate aroma and distinctive character.

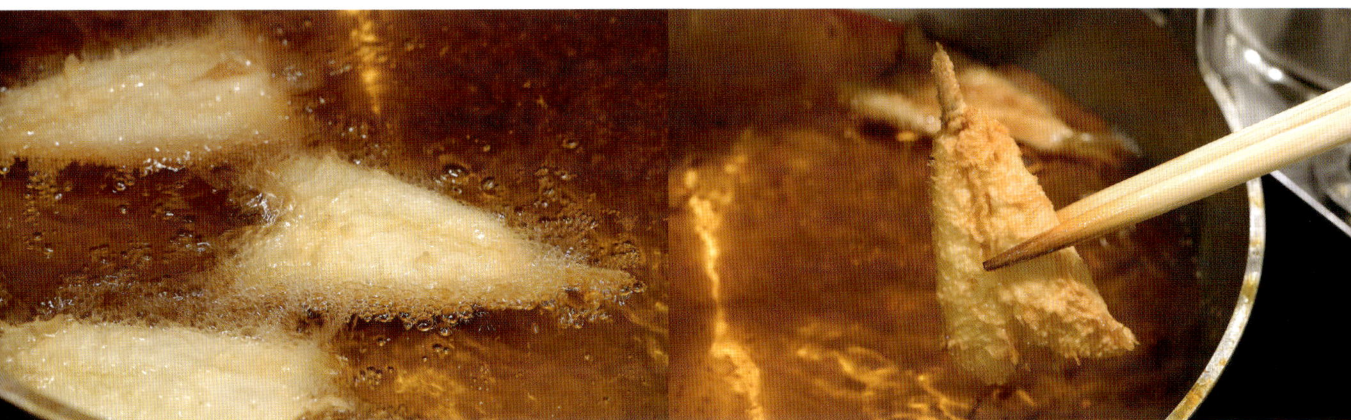

3 When placing it in the oil, make sure the flesh side – which will face up when served – faces up and the skin side faces down.

4 Flip it evenly and take your time to fry it thoroughly.

墨烏賊

Golden Cuttlefish (*Sumi-ika*)

Golden Cuttlefish

Use golden cuttlefish that is fresh enough to be eaten as sashimi. Cut it across the grain to ensure a tender texture. Lightly dust the entire piece with flour, then coat it with batter. To ensure even cooking, fry it while adjusting the time down to the second.

How to Prepare Golden Cuttlefish
➡ page 54

1 Dust the surface evenly with flour. Since the fibers in cuttlefish run horizontally across the body, cut the fillet across the grain.

2 Coat the whole pieces with a fairly thin layer of batter.

Cuttlefish tempura has a graceful curve, and the batter stands up here and there. Its signature qualities are a pleasantly sticky texture and a rich sweetness.

3 Place it in the oil with the outer side — the one that will face up when plated — facing upward. Since it tends to curl, turn it frequently to ensure even cooking throughout.

障泥烏賊

Bigfin Reef Squid (*aori-ika*)

Bigfin Reef Squid

To bring out its sweetness, the squid is rested in the refrigerator before frying. While fresher squid offers more translucence, the distinctive cooked texture and rich flavor develop during this resting period. The resting time depends on the size and firmness of the squid—typically 2–4 days. For a freshly killed bigfin reef squid weighing about 9 lbs (4 kg), it's about 3–4 days. This type of squid is particularly difficult to peel, but the thin outer skin should be thoroughly removed during preparation to prevent oil from splattering. Dust the surface evenly with flour, then coat it with batter so that the thickness is uniform before frying.

How to Prepare Bigfin Reef Squid ➡ page 58

1 Cut the fillet across the squid's grain (see page 61). Dust with flour, then coat evenly with batter. Place in the oil with the gut side down and the outer side up. Cook it while rotating the piece to ensure even frying.

The smooth surface is coated evenly in batter and fried until fine ripples form across the exterior. Tender, springy and sweet, this truly lives up to its reputation as the king of squid.

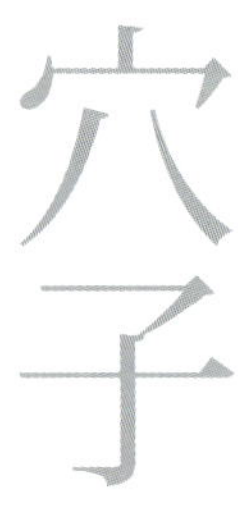

Conger Eel
(*anago*)

Conger Eel

Conger eel is deep-fried whole, using one fillet that's been butterflied along the back. No flour is dusted on beforehand. To keep it from curling or twisting during frying, grip the fillet gently with chopsticks, dip it straight into the batter, then lift it out and place it directly into the oil. When coating it in batter, aim for a thinner layer on the skin side and a slightly thicker one on the flesh side. Place it in the oil skin side down. Fry it at a relatively high temperature until the surface turns crisp and fragrant. When plating, the flesh side—where the batter is thicker than on the skin side—is placed facing up. When cut with metal chopsticks, it should give a satisfying crunch, accompanied by a burst of steam and the uniquely rich aroma of freshly fried conger eel.

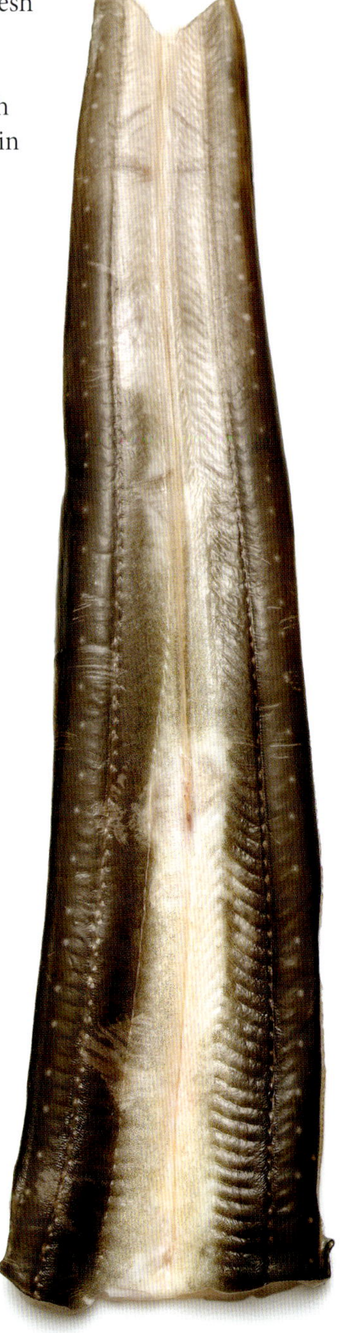

Skin

The skin is composed primarily of collagen. When exposed to heat, the collagen contracts, making the skin thicken and its structure denser. Moisture doesn't escape easily from the skin side, but the flesh side is unprotected and loses moisture more readily. So only a thin layer of batter is applied to the skin side of conger eel, while with fish like whiting (page 128), flour is dusted only on the flesh side. This helps ensure that heat penetration and moisture loss occur evenly throughout the fillet.

How to Prepare Conger Eel ➡ page 46

2 Put the eel straight into the oil with the skin side facing down.

1 Use one whole fillet of conger eel that has been butterflied along the back. Grasp it with chopsticks, skin side facing you, and lower it straight into a slightly thick batter. Be sure to keep the coating thinner on the skin side.

3 Turn the eel over occasionally.

4 Fry thoroughly until the skin is crispy.

At Tempura Nakagawa we slice freshly fried conger eel tempura into two pieces right in front of the customer using metal chopsticks (see page 36). Steam rises from the inside with a sizzling sound and the distinctive aroma of cooked conger eel wafts through the air. Cutting it while it's still piping hot lets excess steam escape, resulting in a tender, fluffy texture.

The Science of Edomae Fish

The Muscles of Edomae Fish

Edo is the old name for Tokyo and the word "Edomae" means "the place in front of Edo," in other words, Tokyo Bay. The term "Edomae fish" refers to fish caught there. The Edo-period document *Buko sanbutsu-shi* (Record of Products of Edo, 1830), listing natural produce found in the Edo area, mentions fish listed in the chart below. Some are red fish like mackerel, but most are white-fleshed varieties. Many of these live on the ocean floor and do not normally swim around much, so they do not require much oxygen to move their muscles. Migratory red fish, however, need oxygen to keep their muscles moving as they continue to swim. Red fish store oxygen in a red pigment called myoglobin, which is why their flesh has a reddish color.

Characteristics of Edomae Fish and Other Fish

Fish name		Fish type	Habitat	Water content (ml)	Protein (g)	Fat (g)
Edomae Fish	Conger eel	White fish	Muddy sandy soil	72.2	17.3	9.3
	Japanese whiting		Sandy soil	80.8	18.5	0.2
	Big-eyed flathead		Muddy sandy soil	81.1	17.1	0.6
	Tidepool gunnel		Muddy sandy soil	–	–	–
	Yellowfin goby		Muddy sandy soil (brackish water zone*)	79.4	19.1	0.2
	Japanese icefish		(brackish water zone*)	82.6	14.0	2.0
Other	Skipjack tuna or bonito	Red fish	Migratory fish	67.3	25.0	6.2
	Mackerel		Migratory fish	62.1	20.6	16.8
	Amberjack		Migratory fish	59.6	21.4	17.6

* Brackish water zone: Brackish water refers to a mixture of fresh water and seawater. A brackish water zone is an area where both types of water intermingle, such as river mouths or coastal waters with freshwater springs.

Tokyo Bay Fish Listed in the 1830 *Record of Products of Edo*

Sea Fish	Black sea bream, striped beakfish, flounder, flathead, mullet, white sardine, juvenile mullet, Japanese sea bass, juvenile Japanese sea bass, young Japanese amberjack, black surfperch, greenling, rockfish, grouper, scorpionfish, white croaker, grunt, horse mackerel, stonefish, white trevally, blue mackerel, gizzard shad, dotted gizzard shad, sardine, yellowfin goby, Japanese whiting, halfbeak, needlefish, Japanese icefish, puffer fish, pike conger, conger eel, red stingray, octopus, Japanese flying squid, jellyfish, sea cucumber, Shiba shrimp, mantis shrimp, mysid shrimp, green sea turtle, blue swimmer crab
Shellfish	Freshwater clam, Asian hard clam, Manila clam, surf clam, scallop, mussel, ark shell, Chinese pond mussel, Japanese whelk, Japanese ivory shell, oyster, river snail 

The Secret to a Tender Texture

The muscle fibers that make up the flesh of a fish consist of jelly-like sarcoplasmic proteins filling the spaces between fibrous myofibrillar proteins (see pages 62–63). White-fleshed and red-fleshed fish differ in the thickness of these muscle fibers, the proportion of sarcoplasmic proteins in the total protein content, and the amount of water they contain. In white-fleshed fish, the muscle fibers are thicker, with a lower proportion of sarcoplasmic proteins and a higher moisture content. As a result, the flesh becomes soft and delicate when cooked, breaking apart easily into flakes.

Red fish has thin muscle fibers, a high percentage of sarcoplasmic reticulum protein, and low water content. When heated, the sarcoplasmic proteins adhere tightly to the myofibrillar proteins, making the flesh firmer and tighter. This is why heated skipjack tuna or *katsuo* becomes *katsuobushi*, (*bushi* meaning "chunk"), the wood-like block of hard fish that is flaked to make dashi stock.

When fish is deep-fried as tempura, the flesh effectively steams inside the batter (page 112). For Edomae white-fleshed fish, as the internal temperature rises during frying, the muscle fibers begin to loosen and the moisture inside the fish turns into steam, which gently lifts and separates the fibers. The result is a light, tender, flaky texture unique to this kind of tempura. When you bite into it, the contrast between the crisp exterior and the soft, airy interior enhances that distinct texture even further.

When the Fish is Being Fried

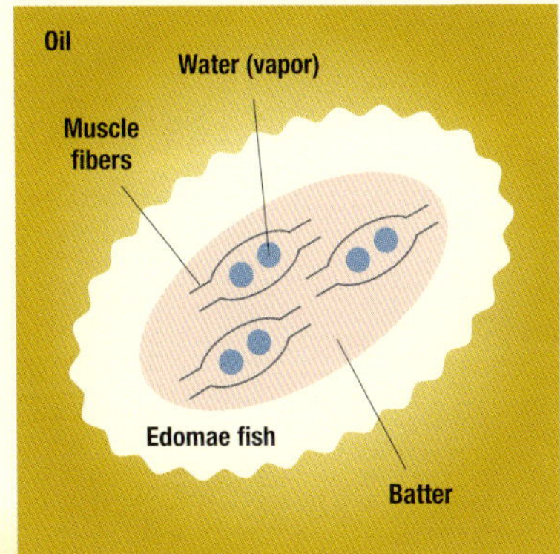

白魚

Japanese Icefish (*shirauo*)

Japanese Icefish

ORDER: Osmeriformes **FAMILY:** Salangidae **SCIENTIFIC NAME:** Salangichthys microdon

This fish is transparent when alive, but turns white after being caught, hence its name. It is often confused with the ice goby, which is a completely different species of fish.

Total length: 4 inches (10 cm) per fish

One of the quintessential signs of spring is icefish. To fry them smoothly, first line them up with their heads facing in the same direction. Coat each evenly with batter, one at a time, and gently place them into the oil head-first, one by one.

1 Hold an icefish by its tail, and dip it in the batter to thinly coat.

2 Hold the fish head-down and quickly place it into the oil so that it lies parallel to the surface.

Although small in size, icefish tempura has a big presence. Beneath its light, crisp texture lies a rich depth of flavor that's hard to imagine from its delicate, translucent appearance.

3 Deep-fry while turning the fish several times.

4 Since multiple pieces are fried in the same oil, remove them with care so that the first and last pieces come out cooked to the same degree.

鱈白子

Cod Milt
(tara shirako)

Cod Milt

Cod milt refers to the sperm sac of the male Pacific cod. A distinctive feature of cod milt is its milky white color and large, lobed shape.

Cod milt has a high amount of moisture, making it a particularly delicate ingredient for tempura. To preserve its rich, creamy texture, don't let too much moisture escape. Lightly dust with flour, coat in a batter with a higher ratio of egg, and cook gently so the heat just reaches the center. Before frying, rinse the milt in soy sauce and cut into individual serving portions.

3½ inches (9 cm)

How to Prepare Cod Milt ➡ page 19

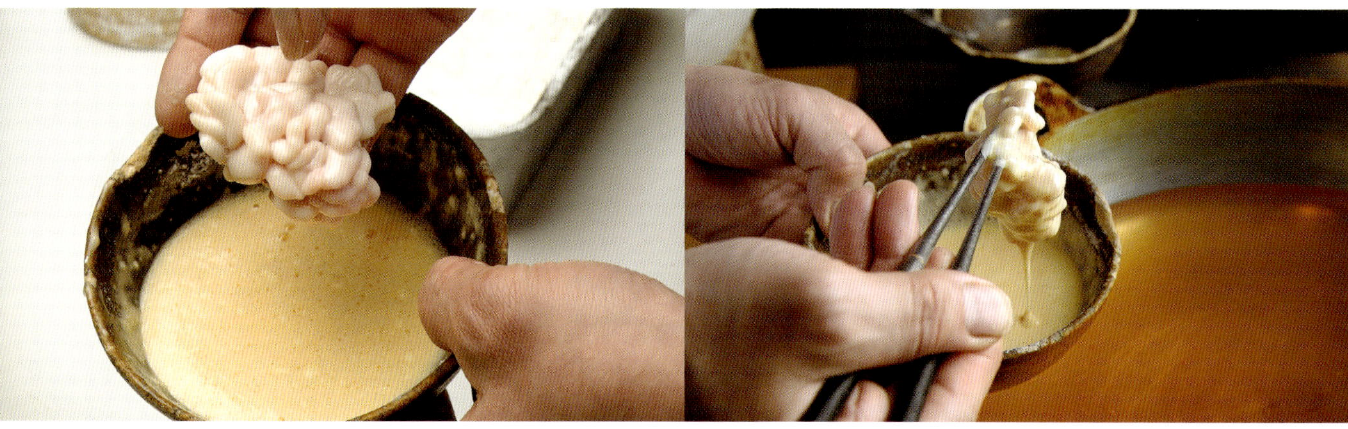

1 Put the batter in a bowl and add extra beaten egg. Dust the milt with flour and coat it with the batter. Check the consistency of the batter and sift in more flour if you want it to be a little thicker.

2 Coat evenly with the batter, and place into the frying oil.

Perfectly cooked cod milt releases its aroma the moment it touches your tongue, filling your mouth with its rich flavor and creamy, custard-like texture. The gentle heat unlocks a depth of character unique to tempura.

3 To avoid concentrating the heat in certain areas and causing the milt to burst, fry it evenly, turning it repeatedly.

河豚白子

Puffer Fish Milt
(*fugu shirako*)

Puffer Fish Milt

Puffer fish milt refers to the sperm sac of a male puffer fish. In the case of the tiger puffer fish, the edible parts are the skin, flesh and milt – none of which contain any toxins.

9½ inches (24 cm)

Winter is the season for tiger puffer fish milt. With its smooth, silky texture and rich flavor, the milt is cut and fried as is. To preserve its distinctive taste, it's lightly dusted with flour, coated in a batter with extra egg, and cooked through gently.

1 Put the batter in a bowl and add extra beaten egg and flour. Dust the milt with flour and coat it with the batter. Check the consistency of the batter and sift in more flour if you want it to be a little thicker.

2 Place in oil and cook evenly, turning over several times.

Underneath the light, yet firm batter is the meltingly tender puffer fish milt. Bite into it while it's still piping hot, and the creamy, subtly sweet flavor fills your mouth. Sprinkle with some sudachi citrus if you like.

Encased in a slightly thicker batter, the milt is fried to a creamy, custard-like finish. It's removed from the oil at just the right moment — when the center is piping hot and gently bubbling.

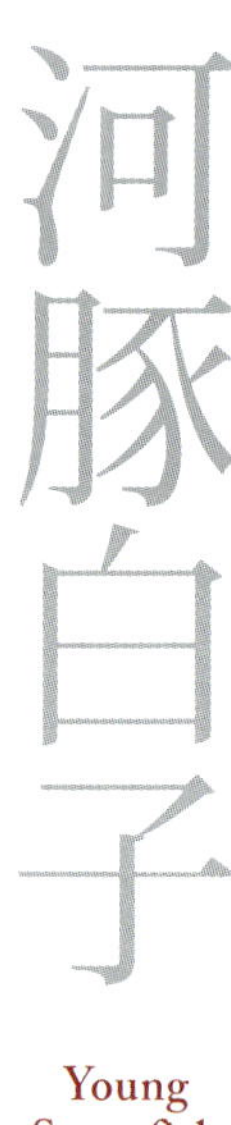

Young Sweetfish (*chiayu*)

Young Sweetfish

ORDER: Osmeriformes **FAMILY:** Plecoglossidae
SCIENTIFIC NAME: Plecoglossus altivelis

Migrates between rivers and the sea. In the ocean, it feeds on zooplankton, but once it enters fresh water, it grazes on algae growing on rocks. Considered a symbolic species of clear mountain streams.

This dish uses juvenile sweetfish raised through a method where young fish are caught in the wild and then cultivated. To preserve the graceful, streamlined shape of each sweetfish even after frying, they are gently placed into the oil one by one, headfirst, as if swimming. Because river fish tend to burn easily, special care is taken to avoid over-browning while still frying the bones and head thoroughly until crisp.

Total length: 4½ inches (11 cm)

1 Lightly dust the thinner-skinned area along the belly with flour.

2 Dip in thin batter 2–3 times.

3 Place each fish into the oil headfirst, as if it were swimming. Fry thoroughly to crisp both the head and bones completely.

The sweetfish is beautifully fried with its distinctive shape perfectly intact. The bones are tender enough to eat whole, and when you bite into it – head, flesh, and even the innards – you'll enjoy a delicate blend of softness, subtle sweetness and a hint of bitterness. Paired with the refreshing aroma of *tade* water pepper vinegar, it evokes the essence of early summer.

Tade dressing

Tade (ta-day) vinegar often accompanies sweetfish dishes. It is made of chopped water pepper leaves, vinegar and salt, and sometimes a few grains of cooked rice to thicken. The sharp aroma, heat and acidity of the vinegar pair beautifully with the rich, slightly bitter flavor of sweetfish. As dipping tempura in vinegar would make the crisp coating soggy, a condiment called *tade-su oroshi* is served instead. This is made by combining minced water pepper leaves with tade vinegar, grated daikon, and salt.

Water pepper is an annual herb of the Polygonaceae family. It grows along riversides and in wetlands. It has a distinctive sharp aroma and spiciness, which comes from a pungent compound known as tadeonal.

岩牡蠣

Japanese Rock Oyster (*iwagaki*)

Japanese Rock Oysters

ORDER: Ostreida **FAMILY:** Ostreidae **SCIENTIFIC NAME:** Crassostrea nippona

This is one of the larger oysters and takes more than three years to grow to fishing size.

3½ x 6 inches (9 x 15 cm)

How to Open Oysters ➡ page 19

Oysters are a summer tempura ingredient and Japanese rock oysters work best—they are large, plump, and can be eaten raw. They're shucked fresh, rinsed in clean water, and patted completely dry before being dusted with flour and lightly fried.

1 Remove the oyster from the shell and blot with kitchen paper to remove excess water.

2 Dust the entire surface with flour.

The rich umami of the oyster is tightly sealed in the batter. The center is kept rare, resulting in a gently warmed, creamy texture. Cooking enhances the oyster's flavor and makes it incredibly juicy. The light batter matches the soft yet rich meat of the rock oyster.

3 Coat the oyster thoroughly in a slightly thick batter with extra egg, then place it in the oil.

4 Deep-fry so that the center remains slightly rare.

Pike Conger
(*hamo*)

Pike Conger

ORDER: Anguilliformes **FAMILY:** Muraenesocidae
SCIENTIFIC NAME: Muraenesox cinereus

Some of the larger pike conger can reach 6 feet (2 meters) in length. A nocturnal carnivore that feeds on small fish, shrimp, squid and octopus.

This tempura ingredient is featured from summer through fall. Pike conger has many fine bones and cannot be eaten without first being carefully cut. This involves making a series of precise incisions through the bones while leaving the skin intact—a highly skilled and specialized technique called *honegiri* in Japanese. For tempura, the pike conger is usually prepared by professional suppliers who expertly handle the cutting to preserve the integrity of the flesh.

1 Dust just the flesh side of the pike conger with flour.

2 Apply batter to the whole fish.

Pike conger tempura has the delicate flavor of white fish, yet with a firmness to the flesh. As it fries, the skin side contracts slightly, causing the fine cuts in the flesh to open up gently – creating a light, airy texture.

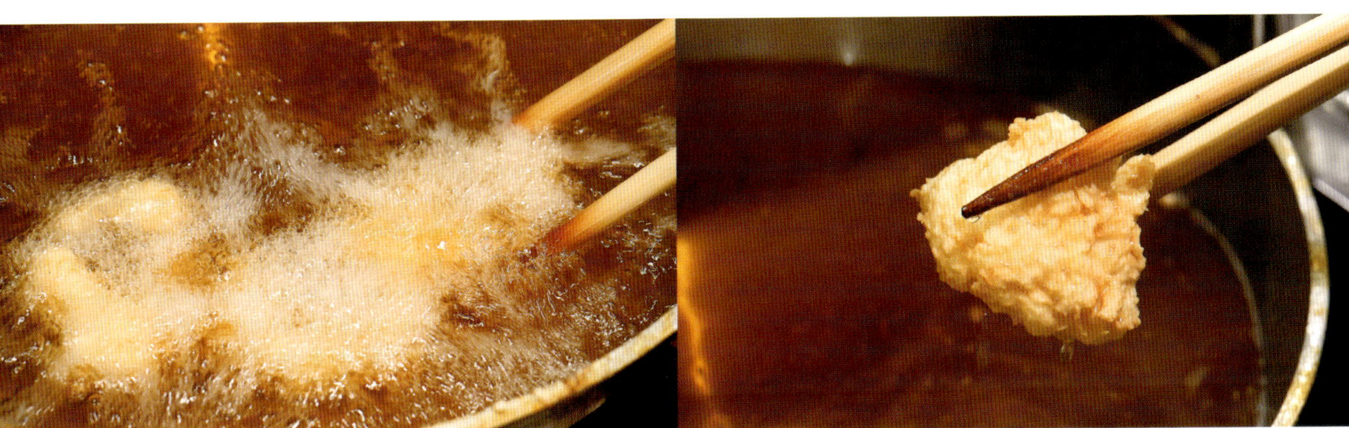

3 Place the fish in the oil skin side down. It will bubble up vigorously.

4 Deep-fry evenly until firm.

Yellowfin Goby
(*haze*)

Yellowfin Goby

Caught from fall into winter, the yellowfin goby has a mild flavor, but as it fattens up, it offers a richer taste than the leaner summer yellowfin goby. Since the white flesh contains a high amount of moisture, it's lightly dusted with flour, then evenly coated in batter before frying. To help remove the excess moisture, it's fried until the coating takes on a slightly deeper golden color.

How to Prepare Yellowfin Goby ➡ page 68

1 Dust only the flesh side of the yellowfin goby with flour.

2 Apply an even layer of fairly thick batter.

This goby tempura is beautifully curled, with the skin side arched upward. As you bite into it, the tender, fluffy flesh breaks apart, offering a balance of delicacy and richness that captures the essence of Edomae fish.

3 Place the fish in the oil with the flesh side up and the skin side down. The photo shows the fish after it has been turned over once (skin side up).

4 Remove it from the oil at the point when just enough moisture has cooked off.

銀宝

Tidepool Gunnel (*ginpo*)

Tidepool Gunnel

The appeal of the tidepool gunnel lies in its supple flesh, gentle sweetness, and delicate ocean aroma. When prepared as tempura, these qualities are fully brought out. Thoroughly crisping the skin enhances its fragrance, while the gelatinous layer between the skin and flesh cooks through, creating a distinctive umami and a pleasantly smooth texture. The fish is carefully turned during frying to ensure it cooks evenly on all sides.

How to Prepare Tidepool Gunnel ➡ page 70

1 Use the base of the knife blade to crush the small bones in the center of the butterflied fish.

2 Lightly dust the area with small bones using a thin layer of flour, then evenly coat the entire piece with a fairly thick batter.

3 Place the fish in the oil with the skin side up and the flesh side down. Deep-fry the fish, frying the flesh side for a bit longer.

The tidepool gunnel is considered a quintessential Edomae tempura ingredient — so much so that it's said you can't truly speak of tempura without having tasted it. Although it has become increasingly rare in recent years due to declining catches, it remains deeply beloved. When fried, its flesh turns fluffy and sweet, giving it a striking presence on the plate.

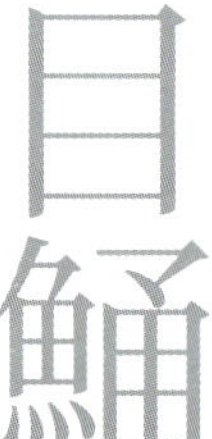

Big-eyed Flathead

When fresh, firm big-eyed flathead is dusted with flour, coated in batter, and placed in the oil, the body spreads open beautifully. Because the fish contains very fine bones, it's important to fry it thoroughly—turning it several times—until a light golden color develops and the bones are crisped up.

Big-eyed Flathead (*megochi*)

How to Prepare Big-eyed Flathead
➡ page 50

1 Dust the whole fish evenly with flour, and shake off the excess.

2 Coat with a fairly thick batter and place it in the oil.

The big-eyed flathead opens up like pine needles as it fries. Thorough frying brings out a toasty aroma that enhances the fish's distinctive flavor, along with its light and refined texture.

3 Fry well, turning several times until well colored on all sides.

雲丹

Sea Urchin
(*uni*)

Sea Urchin

ORDER: Echinoida **FAMILY:** Strongylocentroidae
SCIENTIFIC NAME: Hemicentrotus pulcherrimus

What's sold as shelled meat refers to the reproductive organs (testes or ovaries), which are divided into five lobes that fold inward.

1 piece: 1 x ½ inch (3 x 1 cm)

For this tempura, sea urchin is sandwiched in a green shiso leaf and then deep-fried. If the sea urchin is not firm, it will melt when fried in oil, so select good-quality firm ones. Its sweet, rich umami and briny aroma are sealed inside the batter along with the shiso. To keep the batter from becoming too thick, just a little batter is placed on the inside of the leaf, and then the whole piece is lightly coated in a thin layer of batter. The piece is then gently lowered into the oil to prevent the sea urchin from spilling out.

1 Dust the front side of the shiso leaf with flour.

2 Dip the top half of the leaf in a thin layer of batter.

3 Line up the sea urchin on the unbattered part of the shiso leaf.

4 Cover the sea urchin with the upper half of the shiso leaf.

5 Lightly coat the whole piece with a thin layer of batter.

6 To keep the shiso leaf from opening, gently lower the piece into the oil just above the surface. Remove it once the batter sets and the sea urchin is just gently warmed through.

The vibrant contrast of orange and green is beautifully visible through the light coating. Unlike raw sea urchin, the flavor here becomes concentrated — its distinctive briny richness enveloped by the refreshing aroma of shiso. The difference in how the sea urchin cooks — the parts covered by the leaf compared to the exposed parts — adds depth to both the flavor and texture.

Abalone
(*awabi*)

Abalone

Eaten raw, abalone is crunchy and chewy, but when heated some of the collagen is broken down, giving it a unique tenderness. Simmered abalone requires a long cooking time, but when fried as tempura, cooking time is much shorter and requires careful attention. Since the center contains less collagen and is naturally softer, it's not cooked all the way through—it's gently fried until lightly warmed.

How to Prepare Abalone
➡ page 66

1 Cut the abalone in half. Pat the liver and the body dry using paper towels.

2 Dust the cut surfaces with flour.

Fried to bring out its juicy richness, abalone tempura has a springy, tender texture, with savory juices that seep out as you bite into it. It's cut into generous, bite-size pieces, and served with the liver, which is slightly bitter and deeply flavorful, so you can fully enjoy the briny umami of the sea.

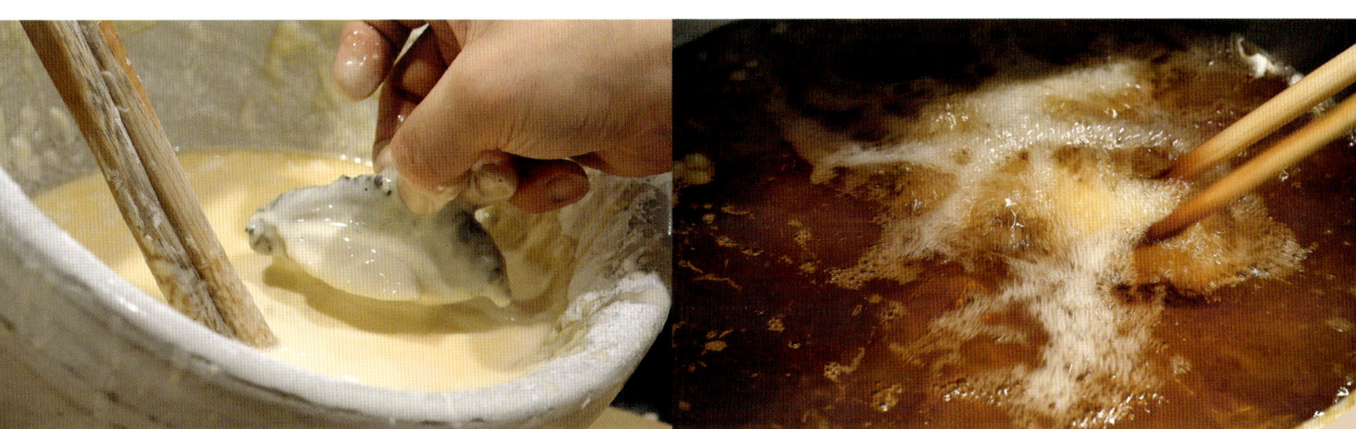

3 Coat the body with a thick batter. Coat the liver in batter too.

4 Place the piece into the oil with the side containing the adductor muscle facing up, and fry evenly on all sides.

Vegetable Tempura

The appeal of vegetable tempura lies in its unique textures and vibrant colors – qualities you won't find in seafood. At Tempura Nakagawa, the freshest seasonal vegetables are carefully sourced, and coated in batter for frying. But the word "vegetables" covers a wide range – from leafy greens like shiso, to vegetables with edible stems like asparagus, to root vegetables like sweet potato – each with different compositions, requiring different frying approaches. Ingredients like spring mountain vegetables and autumn mushrooms are also featured, their natural flavors and even their bitterness sealed in the batter for a rich, full expression of the season.

Our tempura cooking methods bring out the rich aroma and distinctive qualities of each type of vegetable.

銀杏

Ginkgo Nuts
(*ginnan*)

Ginkgo Nuts

Three gingko nuts are dusted with flour, skewered on a hollow pick made of deutzia wood, coated evenly with batter, and deep-fried. The smooth texture and distinctive bitterness of this fall delicacy are unique to the ginkgo nut.

How to Prepare Ginkgo Nuts ➡ page 72

1 Dust the ginkgo nuts lightly with flour.

2 Hold the skewer straight down and dip it into the batter, then draw straight up.

The beautiful jade-green color of the ginkgo nuts can be seen through the batter. The heat brings out their distinctive flavor and pleasantly sticky texture.

3 Remove from the oil when the batter is cooked and fragrant.

万願寺唐辛子

Manganji
Chili Pepper
(*manganji togarashi*)

Manganji Chili Pepper

ORDER: Solanales **FAMILY:** Solanaceae **SCIENTIFIC NAME:** Capsicum annuum

This large, sweet variety of Japanese green pepper was first cultivated in Kyoto. Despite its appearance, it has little to no heat and is prized for its mild flavor.

In summer, these thick, glossy Manganji peppers reach peak flavor. They're fried whole, with a small slit cut into them to prevent them from bursting during cooking.

1 Cut a slit in the pepper to prevent it from bursting

Deep-frying Manganji peppers gives them a lush fresh flavor that is different from that of raw peppers. Frying also creates a vibrant aroma.

2 Coat the pepper with batter without dusting it with flour.

3 Put in oil and deep-fry evenly. When it smells fragrant, take it out of the oil.

薩摩芋

Sweet Potato

ORDER: Solanales **FAMILY:** Convolvulaceae **SCIENTIFIC NAME:** Ipomoea batatas

The Japanese name for this sweet potato, *satsumaimo*, means "Satsuma potato." Satsuma is an old province of southern Japan where the potato was first widely cultivated after being introduced to the country in the seventeenth century.

Sweet Potato (*satsumaimo*)

The sweet potatoes used at Tempura Nakagawa are the Beniazuma variety, known for their fluffy, starchy texture. They're aged for a full year in a *muro* traditional storage room before use. Before frying, they are sliced into ¾ inch (2 cm)-thick rounds. The moisture level at the cut surface is then checked to determine the best frying method. If the slices are especially moist, a dusting of flour is applied, and a lighter batter is used to allow heat to penetrate more easily. They're then fried longer to draw out the moisture and convert the starches into sugars. The rule of thumb: fry until a rich, sweet aroma begins to rise.

Long term storage of sweet potatoes

To preserve sweet potatoes for long periods of time, a traditional curing process is used. When sweet potatoes are harvested, they're vulnerable to spoilage through cuts and abrasions. By placing the freshly dug potatoes in a warm environment, around 86–97°F (30–36°C) with 90–100 percent humidity, a protective corklike layer forms over the cuts, preventing invasion by microbes.

1 Cut the sweet potato into ¾ inch (2 cm) thick slices.

2 Make shallow crisscross cuts into both sides of the slice.

3 Dust the cut sides with flour.

4 Coat evenly with batter before placing in the frying oil.

5 The side that faces down ends up with a thinner coating, while the upper side retains a thicker layer of batter. To ensure even cooking, make sure to fry the thicker side a little longer after flipping.

6 Fry the potatoes thoroughly and evenly until the nutty aroma is released. Depending on the condition of the potatoes, the cooking time should be about 10 minutes after they are placed in 390°F (200°C) oil.

The layer of air between the batter and the sweet potato means that the sweet potato is steamed by its own moisture during the frying process. The texture of sweet potato tempura — crisp on the outside, fluffy on the inside — is distinctly different from that of a baked sweet potato.

Deep-frying Sweet Potato

Aside from its water content, a sweet potato is more than 90 percent starch, and the starch molecules are composed of beads of glucose. Sweet potatoes contain beta-amylase, an enzyme that breaks down starch molecules into sugars, giving the potato its sweetness. However, this enzyme cannot act on raw starch.

When starch is heated in the presence of moisture, it undergoes a process called gelatinization. During this process, the starch absorbs water, becomes translucent and sticky, and forms a gel-like consistency. Beta-amylase can only break down starch once it has been gelatinized.

Sweet potato starch gelatinization occurs at around 150°F (65°C). In other words, it is here that the enzymes begin to work, breaking down the starches into maltose (a sweet sugar consisting of two glucose bonds), which makes the sweet potato sweeter. In tempura, the moisture needed to gelatinize the starch comes from within the sweet potato itself. As it fries, the starch near the surface gelatinizes first, allowing the enzyme to begin converting it to maltose from the outside in. The enzyme stops working at around 165°F (75°C), so sugar production only occurs within the narrow temperature range of 150–165°F (65°C–75°C). The thicker the sweet potato the longer it takes for the temperature in the center to rise, which allows the enzyme more time to work, resulting in a sweeter flavor.

Changes in Temperature of a Sweet Potato

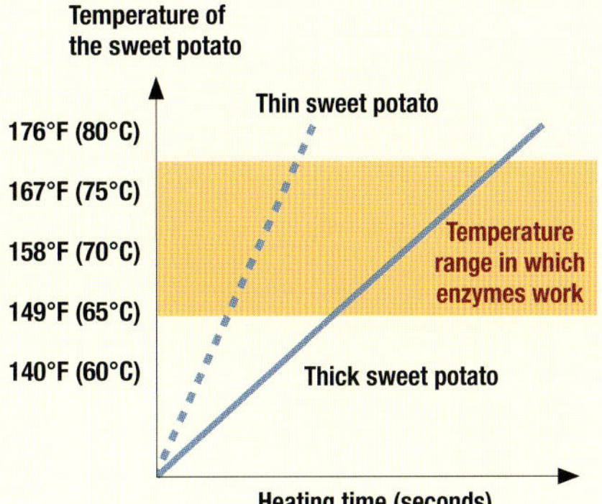

Temperature Changes in the Center of Tempura Nakagawa Sweet Potatoes

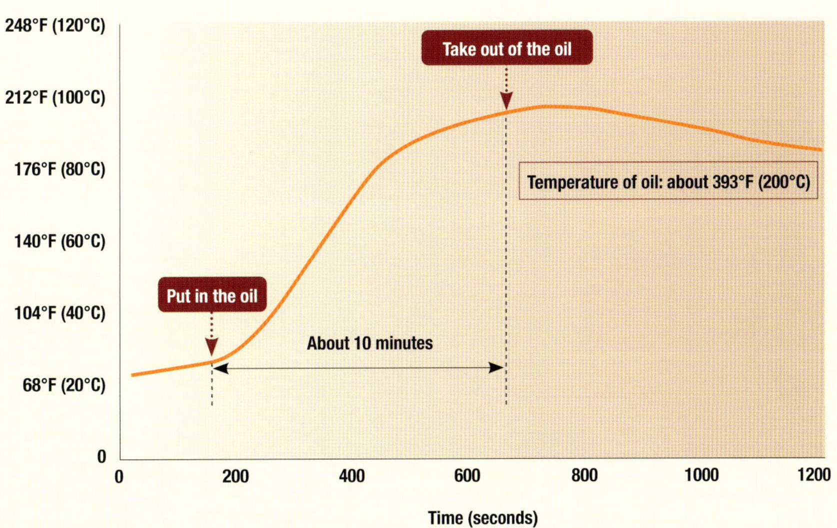

A thermometer was inserted into the center of a sweet potato piece at Tempura Nakagawa to measure changes in internal temperature. Five minutes after being placed in the oil, the center reached 149°F (65°C). After a further 5 minutes the temperature rose to nearly 212°F (100°C), at which point the sweet potatoes were pulled out. (Timing may vary depending on room temperature, the condition of the sweet potato, and other frying conditions.)

Cooperation: Faculty of Health and Nutrition, Bunkyo University

南瓜

Kabocha Squash (*kabocha*)

Kabocha Squash

ORDER: Cucurbitales **FAMILY:** Cucurbitaceae **SCIENTIFIC NAME:** Cucurbita maxima

Kabocha squash is harvested in the summer, but it should be left to mature for about three months because it is watery and has little sweetness immediately after harvest. During the storage period, its starch is converted to sugar, resulting in a sweet, fluffy taste by winter.

When frying, the kabocha squash is cooked slightly longer to allow the starches to convert into sugars, enhancing sweetness, and to draw out moisture for a fluffy texture. However, the oil temperature is kept steady—rather than lowered—and the pieces are gently turned from time to time to ensure they brown evenly without burning.

1 Cut into slices about 1½ inches (3.5 cm) thick, and peel off the skin.

2 Dust the whole piece with flour, and shake off the excess.

The kabocha squash is fried until the starches turn to sugar, yielding a crisp exterior and moist, tender interior. Thick slices are fried whole, then cut into bite-size pieces for serving. The deep orange of the cut surface is glossy and vibrant, hinting at the rich, velvety texture.

3 Coat with batter and put into the oil.

4 Fry until the surface is browned. Cut into bite-size pieces after frying.

アスパラガス

Asparagus
(*asuparagasu*)

Asparagus

ORDER: Asparagales **FAMILY:** Asparagaceae **SCIENTIFIC NAME:** Asparagus officinalis L.

Asparagus has both female and male plants. Female plants produce thicker, higher-quality stalks but yield fewer of them. Male plants grow thinner stalks but produce more shoots, resulting in a higher overall yield.

When frying asparagus, the goal is to highlight its natural aroma and texture. To achieve this, the batter should coat the surface only lightly. This thin, crisp layer adds a toasty flavor while allowing the tender, fluffy texture of perfectly fried asparagus to shine. As the tips and stalk ends cook at different rates, the asparagus is cut into sections, with small slits made in each section to ensure even cooking.

1 Cut off the bottom 1 inch (3 cm) and discard. Cut the remaining stalk in half. Make deep slits in the lower half.

2 Make shallow cuts in the top half. Dust only cut surfaces with flour and coat the asparagus with thin batter. Drop the pieces into the hot oil, turning as they fry. Remove when fragrant.

With each bite, the asparagus yields with a soft fluffiness, releasing a burst of fresh vegetable juice. The crisp batter adds a satisfying contrast, leaving behind the lingering, distinctive pleasure that only tempura can offer.

モロッコ隠元

Flat Green Beans
(*morokko ingen*)

Flat Green Beans

ORDER: Fabales **FAMILY:** Fabaceae **SCIENTIFIC NAME:** Phaseolus vulgaris L.

Characterized by their flat, broad shape, these beans are also called *sandomame* – "three-time beans" – in Japanese because they can be harvested three times a year. However, their true peak season is summer.

This is a type of flat green bean which is eaten whole, pod and all. It's prized for its crisp texture and gentle sweetness. Shallow slits are cut into the pod, then it's coated in a light batter and fried until just slightly browned.

The beans are wrapped in a thin, crispy batter. Deep-frying brings out the sweetness and aroma. The crispy, juicy texture lingers in the mouth.

1 Trim off the ends of the bean pods and cut each into 2 equal pieces.

2 Without removing the string, make a few shallow slits along each pod. Coat lightly in batter and place in the oil. Fry until just slightly browned, then remove.

茄子

Eggplant
(*nasu*)

Eggplant

ORDER: Solanales **FAMILY:** Solanaceae **SCIENTIFIC NAME:** *Solanum melongena*

Eggplant is in season in summer when it has a slightly thicker skin to resist the heat.

This vegetable has a distinctive bitterness, but frying at high heat softens that bitterness, enhances its sweetness, and brings out its full flavor. Shallow slits are cut into the surface, then the eggplant is coated evenly in batter—without any flour dusting—and fried thoroughly while turning, until lightly browned.

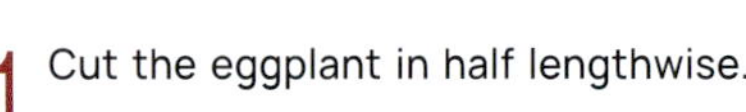

1 Cut the eggplant in half lengthwise.

2 Cut each half in half again lengthwise, and make 3-4 shallow knife marks into the eggplant parallel to the cut.

The deep purple hue showing through the batter is striking. The skin side is coated with a thinner layer of batter, while a slightly thicker coating is left on the flesh. This contrast creates a crisp surface and a meltingly tender interior.

3 Coat the piece with a thin layer of batter.

4 Put the piece in the oil from the skin side, and fry while turning until fragrant.

コロス

Pearl Onion
(*pekorosu*)

Pearl Onion

ORDER: Asparagales **FAMILY:** Amaryllidaceae **SCIENTIFIC NAME:** Allium cepa "pekorosu"

These small onions are cultivated by densely planting regular onion varieties.

The pearl onions soften when cooked. They are cut in half before frying. Because the batter can slip off easily, the cut sides are dusted with flour, then coated with a thin layer of batter and gently lowered into the oil. They're fried slowly until the cut surfaces turn a light golden brown.

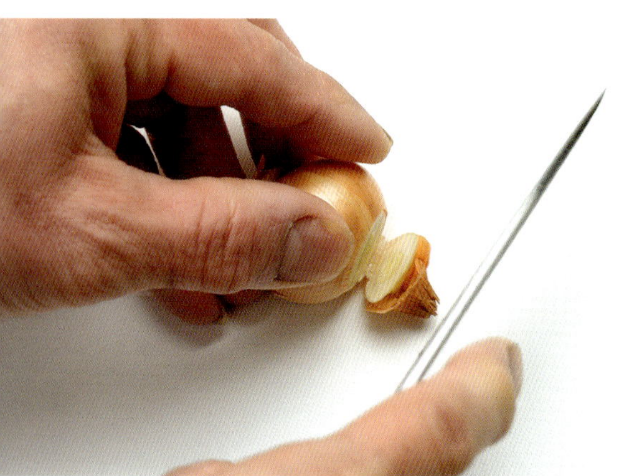

1 Trim off the ends of the pearl onion, and peel off the skin.

2 Cut in half lengthwise.

The small, bite-size onions are slowly cooked to a sweet, crunchy texture. The slight charring on the cut edges adds a nice accent to the dish.

3 Dust the cut sides with flour.

4 Lightly coat with a slightly thick batter and place in the oil with the cut side facing up. Fry slowly until evenly cooked and lightly browned.

蓮根

Lotus Root
(*renkon*)

Lotus Root

ORDER: Proteales **FAMILY:** Nelumbonaceae **SCIENTIFIC NAME:** Nelumbo nucifera

Lotus root is the underground stem of the lotus plant, found underwater. Once moisture is removed, it's made up of about 80 percent starch.

Lotus root fried as tempura is a traditional Zen Buddhist vegetarian food. It is prized for the variety of textures it can offer—sticky, fluffy or crisp—depending on its quality and how it's cooked. Here, thick slices are given a light coating of batter and fried slowly to bring out a crisp bite and subtle sweetness. It is cut just before frying and not soaked in water to remove bitterness, allowing its distinctive flavor to shine through.

1 Just before frying, slice the lotus root into ½ inch (1.5 cm)-thick rounds and peel.

2 Dust both cut sides with flour.

The distinctive shape of the lotus root, with its natural holes, remains beautifully intact. With each crisp bite, you taste the fresh juiciness unique to lotus root, along with the subtle sweetness brought out by the heat.

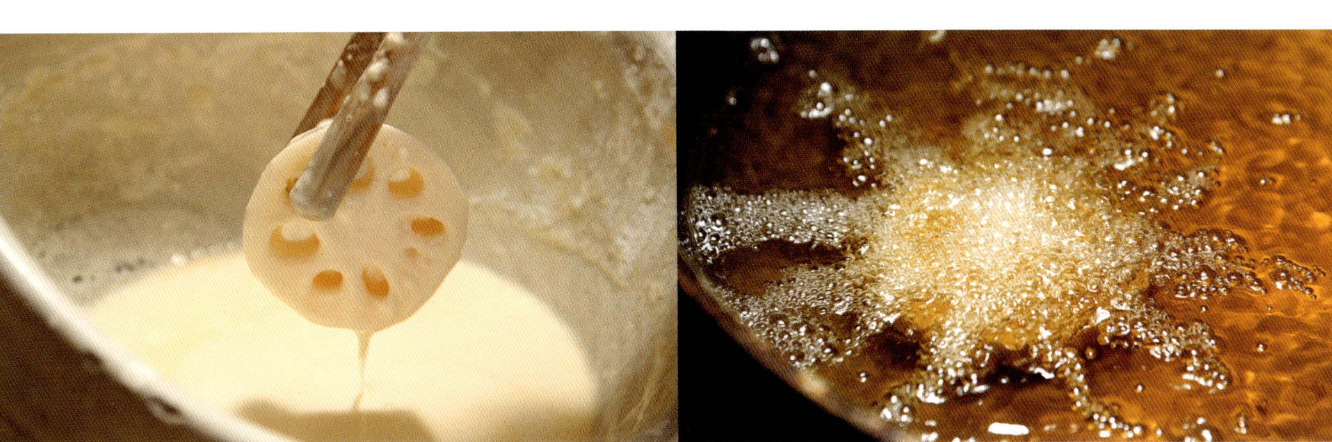

3 Coat the whole slice with batter.

4 Put into the oil. Turn over several times to ensure it cooks evenly.

谷中生姜

Young Ginger

ORDER: Zingiberales **FAMILY:** Zingiberaceae
SCIENTIFIC NAME: Zingiber officinale

This is young leaf ginger harvested early while the rhizome is still small and tender, with the leafy stalks left attached.

Young Ginger (*yanaka shoga*)

Young ginger is a traditional Tokyo vegetable, with its peak season in summer. It has a mild yet sharp heat and a clean, refreshing finish. A dollop of Shinshu miso is inserted into a cut in the stalk, then the whole piece is coated in a slightly thick batter and fried, to seal in its fresh, juicy flavor.

Shinshu miso

A miso made from rice malt and soybeans, Shinshu miso has a light color and a fairly salty taste.

1 If there are any side protrusions, trim them off with a knife to create a slender, uniform shape. Slice about 1–2 mm off the tip.

2 Using the flat side of the knife blade, gently tap shallow slits into both sides of the ginger. Then make a vertical cut lengthwise along the bottom of the stalk.

With the first bite, juice bursts out as a refreshing aroma rises, followed by the rich umami of Shinshu miso spreading across the palate.

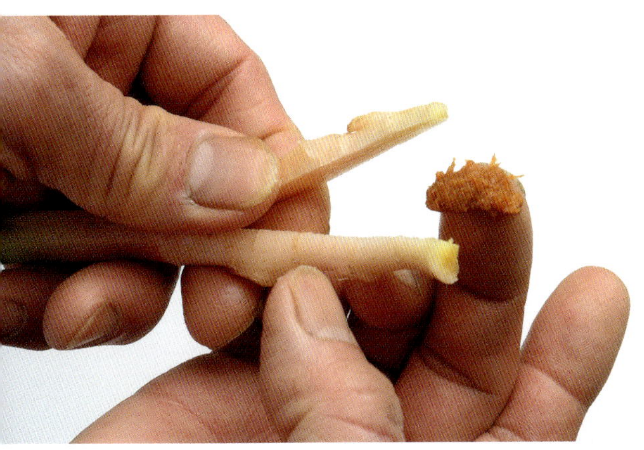

3 Just before frying, insert the Shinshu miso paste between the incision at the bottom of the stalk.

4 The portion of ginger shoot stuffed with miso is coated with batter and deep-fried.

How to Deep-fry Wild Mountain Vegetables and Matsutake Mushrooms

In spring it might be mountain vegetables, in autumn, matsutake mushrooms – each season offers tempura ingredients you can only enjoy at that moment. Their fleeting availability leaves a vivid impression, stirring a desire to taste them again the following year. You find yourself counting down the months.

The fresh bitterness of spring and the deep fragrance of autumn are sealed inside a delicate coating of batter and fried with care. Rising aromas, the movement of fine bubbles in the oil, the feel of the ingredient when touched with cooking chopsticks – all five senses are engaged. With the passing year in mind, the perfect moment to lift each piece from the oil is chosen with utmost attention.

の
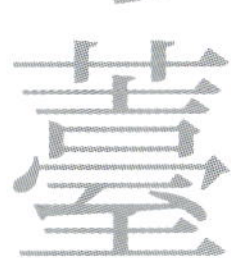

Butterbur Buds
(*fuki no to*)

Butterbur Buds

ORDER: Asterales **FAMILY:** Asteraceae **SCIENTIFIC NAME:** Petasites japonicus

This ingredient is the flower bud of the butterbur plant. After the bud blooms, the plant produces long stalks and broad leaves, which are also edible and known as butterbur.

The buds are valued for their distinctive, pleasantly bitter flavor. However, when deep-fried whole, that bitterness can be too intense and overwhelming. To avoid this, the tightly packed outer layers of the bud are gently opened before cooking. A light dusting of flour is applied to the center, then a thin layer of batter. Because the bud is delicate and prone to burning, it's fried slowly and carefully, turning gently to ensure it cooks evenly without charring.

1 If the base of the butterbur bud is blackened, cut it off and remove the outermost layers.

2 Cut off the tip.

3 Open up the outer layers.

4 Gently open the outer layers fully, so that the bud is fully exposed and faces forward.

5 Dust the bud only with flour.

6 Hold the bud and coat only the opened outer layers with batter, leaving the bud itself uncoated.

7 Put into the oil gently, with the opened outer layers first.

8 Deep-fry the bud evenly, turning it carefully to avoid burning. When a slight aroma emerges, remove it from the oil.

Tempura made with opened butterbur buds is visually striking, with the unfurled outer layers creating a delicate, flower-like shape. The bitterness is pleasantly mellowed, allowing the fresh, springlike aroma to come through. The thinly battered outer leaves fry up light and crispy, adding texture and flavor to each bite.

山独活

Japanese Udo
(*yama-udo*)

Japanese Udo

ORDER: Apiales **FAMILY:** Araliaceae **SCIENTIFIC NAME:** Aralia cordata

Only the young shoots that have just emerged from the soil are used for eating.

There are two main types of Japanese udo (also called Japanese spikenard): in addition to wild varieties, there is *yama-udo* which is cultivated with some exposure to light and has a slightly greenish color. Then there is *nanpaku-udo* which is cultivated in the dark and not exposed to light. Wild udo has a subtle bitterness and crisp, refreshing texture. While it has a strong astringency, this is mellowed through frying, so it is not pretreated to remove bitterness—instead, its bold character is embraced as part of its appeal.

1 Separate the root part from the leaf part, trimming off the hard end of the root. Cut the root part into bite-size pieces.

2 Peel the root part.

Root and leaves are fried separately. The roots are crunchy and the leaves have a unique aroma. A gentle, springlike bitterness lingers pleasantly on the palate.

3 Make shallow incisions all around the stem by lightly tapping with the blade of a knife. Dredge the stem in batter without dusting first with flour.

4 Because the root and leaf cook at different rates, the root is added to the oil first, followed by the leaf a short time later. Each is removed once its aroma begins to rise.

こごみ

Fiddlehead Fern (*kogomi*)

Fiddlehead Fern

ORDER: Polypodiales **FAMILY:** Onocleaceae
SCIENTIFIC NAME: Matteuccia struthiopteris

This perennial is commonly known English as the fiddlehead fern. Specifically, it refers to the young shoots of the ostrich fern, which are called *kogomi* in Japanese.

These spring mountain vegetables are especially popular because of their mild flavor and low bitterness—they're even said to be safe to eat raw in small amounts when freshly picked. To preserve their delicate taste and tender-crisp texture, they're coated lightly in batter and fried for just a short time.

1 Trim off the base of the stems. Place the ferns in a bowl of water and gently pull apart each coiled tip slightly, washing it carefully with your fingers. Pat dry, then without dusting with flour, coat the entire fern lightly in batter. Place in the oil and fry, turning several times, until a fragrant aroma begins to rise.

Tempura made with fiddlehead ferns has a charming appearance. Beneath the light, crisp coating, a delicate springlike bitterness and fresh aroma emerge with each bite.

松茸

Matsutake Mushrooms (*matsutake*)

Matsutake Mushrooms

ORDER: Agaricales **FAMILY:** Tricholomataceae
SCIENTIFIC NAME: Tricholoma matsutake

Matsutake mushrooms grow in red pine forests, and in stands of black pine and other trees. When the cap is still tightly closed, it's called a *koro*. As it grows, the name changes with its stage of development – *tsubomi* (bud), *nakahiraki* (half-open), and *hiraki* (fully open).

When it comes to the king of autumn flavors, nothing tops the matsutake mushroom. Its most prized feature is its unmistakable aroma. Choose mushrooms with unopened caps, coat them whole in batter, and fry quickly in hot oil to lock in their fragrance. But the matsutake isn't just about scent—it's also celebrated for its rich flavor and firm texture. Frying helps draw out excess moisture, concentrating the umami and tightening the flesh. However, overcooking will dry it out, so it's important to watch closely and remove the mushroom from the oil just as the aroma begins to emerge—capturing it at the perfect moment.

1 Shave the base of the stem to a tapered point, like the tip of a pencil. Then make a shallow cut about ¾ inch (2 cm) long from the base upward toward the cap.

2 Make a shallow cut about ¾ inch (2 cm) long from the cap down toward the base of the stem.

Split the mushroom in half with chopsticks along the place where you made the cuts in Step 1 and Step 2, to release the aroma. The pleasantly springy texture, with just the right amount of moisture, adds to the luxurious flavor – an unmistakable taste of fall.

3 Dip the whole matsutake mushroom in batter.

4 Deep-fry the matsutake mushroom in slightly hotter oil than usual, and cook until fragrant.

舞茸

Maitake Mushrooms (*maitake*)

Maitake Mushrooms

ORDER: Polyporales **FAMILY:** Meripilaceae **SCIENTIFIC NAME:** Grifola frondosa

Also known as "hen of the woods," maitake mushrooms grow at the base or on the stumps of old broadleaf trees such as beech, oak and cherry. Their branching caps overlap and cluster together, forming large, layered masses.

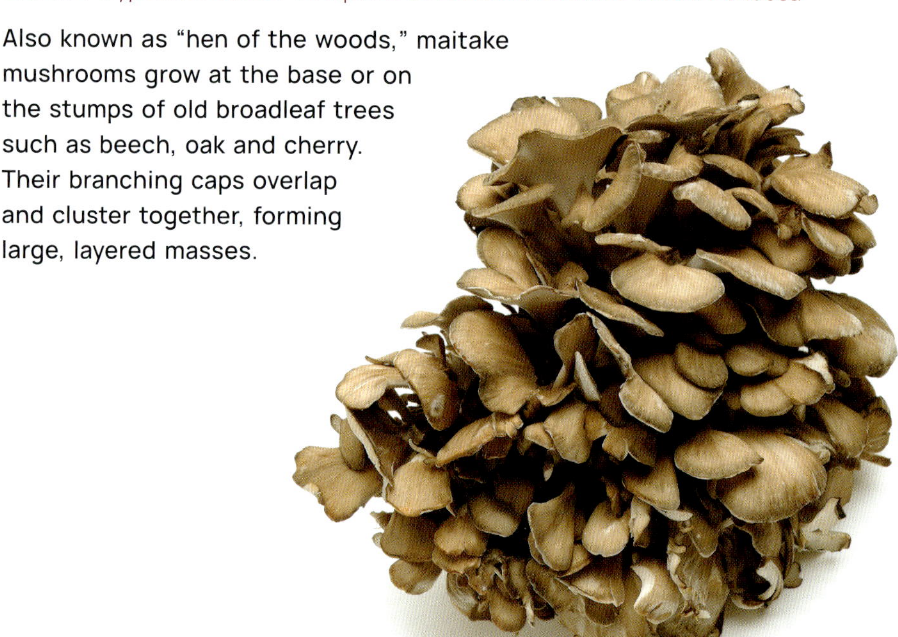

Mushrooms contain a lot of moisture, so they're fried in a way that seals that moisture inside. For maitake, batter tends to collect where the overlapping caps meet, so excess batter should be shaken off to allow each cap to open up beautifully during frying. Fry briefly at high heat for the best texture and flavor.

1 Make a small cut at the base of each clump with a knife, and tear apart by hand.

2 Dip the entire piece in the batter. Shake off the excess batter, holding the mushroom piece upside down so that batter does not collect between the caps.

Each petal-like cap emerges from the oil with a delicate, even coating of batter. Beneath the light, crisp texture, the mushroom's juicy essence bursts forth, filling the mouth with its fresh, savory flavor.

3 Put the mushroom piece in the high temperature oil, cap side first. Any excess batter on the caps will fall off at this stage.

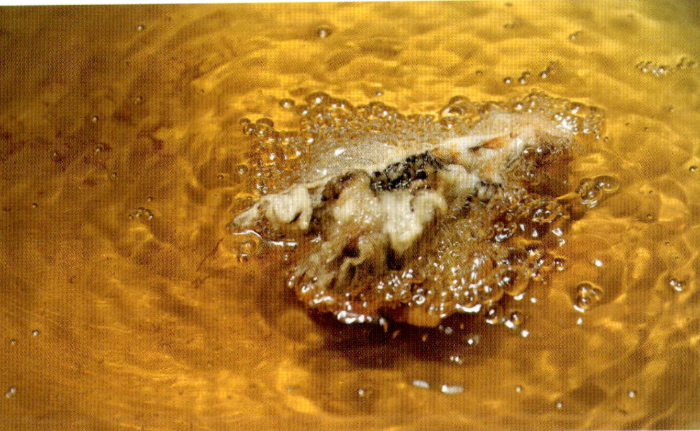

4 Deep-fry until crispy all over.

The Tempura Frying Process

Tempura fried at high heat requires precise control over how the heat transfers to the ingredient. The goal is to cook it through – not too much, not too little – so it's essential that the process from dipping it in batter to placing it in the oil flows smoothly and without hesitation. During frying, full attention is focused on the pot: the sound, the movement and bubbling of the oil, and closely observing how the ingredient changes. The aim is to lift it out at the perfect moment. Here, we demonstrate the process using a tiger shrimp.

Prepare the ingredients. Peel the tiger shrimp just before frying. Here, two shrimp will be fried at the same time.

Stretch out the tiger shrimp bodies so that they do not curl up while being fried.

Hold one tiger shrimp in each hand, and first dip the shrimp in the dominant hand in the batter. Place the shrimp vertically in the batter so that the batter does not stick to the shrimp too much.

As soon as the first tiger shrimp is coated with batter, place it in the oil.

Coat the other tiger shrimp with batter in the same way and place in the oil.

Keep a close eye on the tiger shrimp as they fry. Turn them over once.

The tiger shrimp are done about 30 seconds after putting in the oil.

Shake the fried tiger shrimp above the pot to remove excess oil, and place on the customer's paper-lined plate right away.

CHAPTER 7

KAKIAGE MIXED FRITTERS

"Perfect tempura is all about timing—
knowing exactly when the heat has done its job."

—Chef Takashi Nakagawa

Scallops

ORDER: Venerida **FAMILY:** Mactridae **SCIENTIFIC NAME:** Mactra chinensis

The Japanese surf clam is usually sold with the body and adductor muscle separated. The shucked clam meat is called *aoyagi*, while the adductor muscle is called *kaibashira*, which is translated here as "scallop."

Scallops (*kaibashira*)

There are two types of scallops, large and small. In specialty stores in Japan, the larger scallops are called *mesuboshi* ("female stars") and the smaller ones are called *osuboshi* ("male stars"). Female stars are considered to have superior sweetness, umami, and texture. However, the two types are typically mixed together when sold.

Kakiage is a mixed tempura fritter, often made by combining various ingredients, but at Tempura Nakagawa, kakiage is made with a single ingredient: scallops. According to Chef Takashi Nakagawa, this is the most technically challenging tempura to fry. The scallops are gathered into a cluster and coated in a slightly thicker batter, which tends to cook unevenly. To achieve a perfect fry, it's essential to consider the "heat pathways" or the flow of heat through the food. If there are areas on the kakiage where no bubbles are appearing in the oil, this means that those areas are likely to be undercooked. When this happens, Chef Nakagawa gently inserts chopsticks into the kakiage to open a path for the heat to reach those spots. Achieving a crispy coating while keeping the scallop centers rare—and doing so evenly—requires intense focus and expert skill.

The scallop is the muscle a clam uses to close its shell. Clams have two of these muscles – one at the front and one at the back. In the Japan the larger scallop (left) is referred to as the "female star," while the smaller one (right) is called the "male star."

1 Put the scallops in a bowl with the batter and mix. Add more beaten egg.

2 Add more sifted flour to the Step 1 mixture.

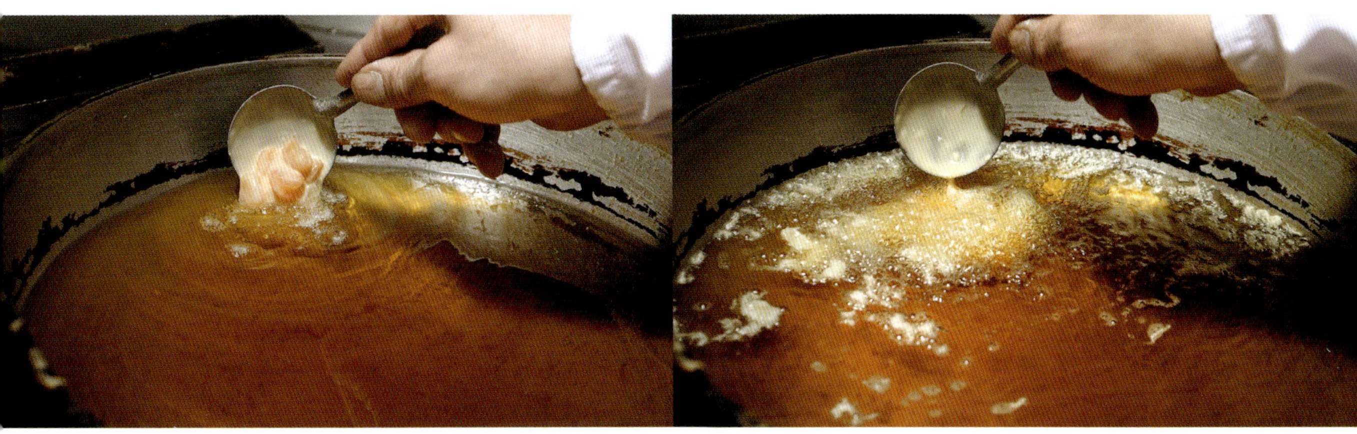

3 Scoop up the batter-coated scallops in a ladle, and place them in slightly cooler oil. The kakiage fritter will sink when you first put it in, but will come floating up right away.

4 When bubbles begin to form, add a ladleful of batter on top. As soon as it starts to take shape, hold the edges with chopsticks and turn the kakiage over.

5 Deep-fry while observing the balance between the upper and lower batter. When the batter at the center is cooked through, remove the kakiage from the pot.

6 This is the finished kakiage. The batter is light and airy, with a crisp, delicate texture, while the inside is cooked to medium-rare, preserving the tender juiciness of the shellfish.

This beautifully round kakiage is a showcase of expert technique. In the brief time it spends in the oil, the chef must shape it carefully to keep it from falling apart, while also judging the precise amount of heat needed – ensuring the kakiage is neither undercooked nor overdone. This dish is the true test of the skill of a tempura chef.

TECHNIQUE FOCUS

The Front and Back Sides of Tempura

Tempura has a "front" and a "back." The front is the side that faces up when plated; the back is the side that rests on the plate. Which side is the front is determined from the moment the batter is applied. As a general rule, the front-facing side should be positioned upward when coating with batter, and then placed into the oil with that same side facing up. When batter is applied to both sides and the ingredient is slid into the oil, some batter naturally falls off the underside. Also, the way the batter clings and spreads differs between the top and bottom surfaces during frying, which affects the final shape and texture of the coating. The top side tends to develop a more textured appearance, which is why it's presented as the front. Taking these differences in batter behavior into account, the chef visualizes how the heat will flow and how the final coating will look while carrying out each step.

The shape of the tempura is determined the moment it is placed in the oil. The batter on the top side becomes three-dimensional and forms the "front" of the tempura.

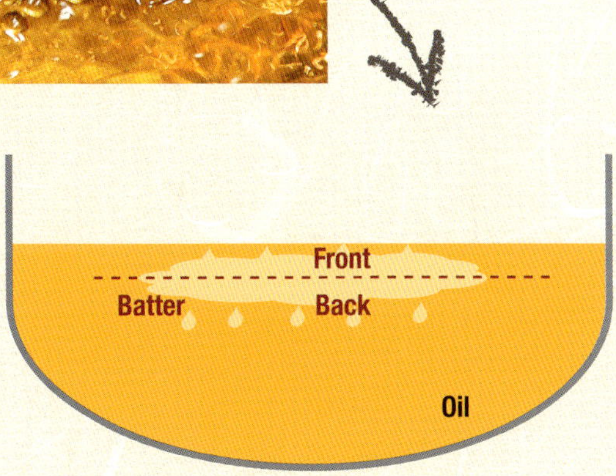

芝海老

Small White Shrimp

ORDER: Decapoda **FAMILY:** Penaeidae **SCIENTIFIC NAME:** *Metapenaeus joyneri*

In some regions of Japan, these small shrimp are sometimes called *akahige* ("red whiskers") because their antennae are red. The body surface is rough to the touch with irregular shallow indentations and fine, stiff hairs.

Small White Shrimp (*shiba ebi*)

Tempura Nakagawa's kakiage fritters are usually made with scallops, but during periods when scallops are not available, small white shrimp make their appearance. They are called *shiba ebi* in Japanese because they were once caught off the Shiba coast of Tokyo Bay. The blue-white body has numerous fine dark green spots. The more clearly defined these spots are, the fresher and higher in quality the shrimp is considered to be.

At Tempura Nakagawa, the shells are removed and only the meat is used for kakiage. In order to keep the shrimp fresh, the shells are peeled quickly and with minimal handling to prevent the heat of the hands from being transferred to the delicate flesh.

To bring out the shrimp's signature springy texture and sweetness, the batter contains extra egg, which helps the shrimp cook gently. As the kakiage fries, it is quickly shaped into a neat circle with chopsticks and flipped swiftly so that it maintains its form and holds everything together.

1 Insert your thumb into the back of the head of the shrimp and twist to remove it. At the same time, the vein along the back will come out, so remove that as well.

2 Peel off the legs from the side of the shell.

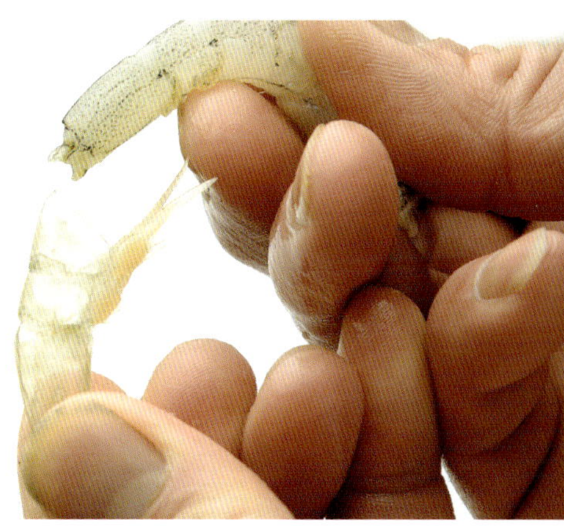

3 Remove the legs from the head part and the abdomen.

4 Pull off the tail and remove the shell.

Peeled white shrimp. The peeled shrimp are placed in a container in the refrigerator. Take them out of the refrigerator just before frying.

5 Place the peeled shrimp in a bowl and add the batter.

6 Add some more beaten egg.

7 Sift in some more flour.

8 Coat the shrimp evenly with batter. Use the curve of the bowl to scoop out a well-rounded portion with a ladle.

9 Put a ladleful of the shrimp-and-batter mixture into the oil.

10 Deep-fry while forming the kakiage into a round. When the batter at the center is cooked through, remove the kakiage from the oil.

When scallops are out of season, Tempura Nakagawa uses small white shrimp for kakiage. Their vivid red color when cooked shows through the batter, making for a striking presentation. Kakiage is a great way to highlight the natural sweetness and springy texture of small white shrimp.

The Final Course

At Tempura Nakagawa, the kakiage is served in one of three styles, depending on the customer's choice: as a teishoku set meal with rice and miso soup, as a tendon tempura rice bowl with sauce poured over, or as tencha tempura over rice with hot broth poured on top.

Our miso soup recipe

A miso soup base is made by mixing Hatcho miso and Shinshu miso at a 7:3 ratio in dashi stock. When an order comes in for miso soup, Japanese freshwater clams (*shijimi*) are added and warmed through.

八丁味噌

Hatcho Miso

Hatcho miso is made from only soybeans, salt and koji, and uses soybean koji instead of the usual rice koji used to make miso. It is matured for one to three years, resulting in a rich, dark red miso. It is made only in the Tokai region of central Japan.

蜆

Shijimi Clams

These clams live in fresh water and brackish water. They're rich in natural umami compounds, including succinic acid—one of the key elements that gives shellfish their savory depth. They also contain nutrients that support liver health.

Teishoku Set Meal

The freshly fried kakiage is plated and served with rice, miso soup and house-made pickles. The crisp batter of the kakiage and the tender, slightly rare center of the scallops can be enjoyed just as they are.

Tendon Rice Bowl

How to Make Tendon Sauce

Dashi stock (see page 102)
Mirin
Soy sauce
Leftover tentsuyu from the day before (see page 102)

1 Combine the dashi stock, mirin and soy sauce in a 1 : 1 : 0.7 ratio.
2 Simmer the Step 1 mixture until reduced to one third its original volume.
3 Mix the Step 2 sauce with the previous day's tentsuyu at a 1 : 1 ratio.

The kakiage is briefly dipped in tendon sauce and then placed on top of a bowl of rice. The sauce gently soaks into the crisp batter and blends beautifully with the freshly cooked rice, making even the sauce-soaked grains a pleasure to eat. Served with miso soup and house-made pickles.

Tencha Tempura on Rice with Dashi Stock

Freshly fried kakiage is placed on a bowl of rice and dashi stock is poured over. (Use your favorite dashi – ours is made with Rishiri kombu and bonito flakes.) It is garnished with freshly grated wasabi and mitsuba leaves. This dish is enjoyed by savoring the refined dashi along with its "main ingredients" – the rice and kakiage. Served with house-made pickles on the side.

Oil Disposal

After frying tempura, you're left with used oil—which can't simply be poured down the drain. In home kitchens in Japan, people typically dispose of it by soaking it up with newspaper or old magazines, or by pouring it into an empty milk carton or plastic bag, or solidifying it with a coagulant. Some municipalities also encourage oil recycling.

At professional tempura restaurants, however, the volume of oil used is far greater, and the amount of waste oil generated is on a completely different scale from that of home cooking. Most restaurants collect this used oil and arrange for specialized disposal services. These companies recycle the oil into products like animal feed, fertilizer, paint and soap.

Tempura Nakagawa
2-14-2 Tsukiji, Chuo-ku, Tokyo, Japan

Index

"Books to Span the East and West"

Tuttle Publishing was founded in 1832 in the small New England town of Rutland, Vermont [USA]. Our core values remain as strong today as they were then—to publish best-in-class books which bring people together one page at a time. In 1948, we established a publishing outpost in Japan—and Tuttle is now a leader in publishing English-language books about the arts, languages and cultures of Asia. The world has become a much smaller place today and Asia's economic and cultural influence has grown. Yet the need for meaningful dialogue and information about this diverse region has never been greater. Over the past seven decades, Tuttle has published thousands of books on subjects ranging from martial arts and paper crafts to language learning and literature—and our talented authors, illustrators, designers and photographers have won many prestigious awards. We welcome you to explore the wealth of information available on Asia at **www.tuttlepublishing.com**.

Published by Tuttle Publishing, an imprint of Periplus Editions (HK) Ltd.

www.tuttlepublishing.com

Tempura no Science: Oishisa wo Tsukuridasu Riron to Gijutsu ga Mieru

Staff for the Japanese edition:
Photography: Ryoichi Yamashita
Design: Miho Takahashi
Special thanks to Yumiko Ito, Chiyoko Iijima for help with the editing
Special thanks to Bunkyo University Faculty of Health and Nutrition
Special thanks to OKAMURA OIL MILL, LTD., Noi Maeshige

ISBN: 978-4-8053-1912-3

Distributed by:
North America, Latin America & Europe
Tuttle Publishing
364 Innovation Drive
North Clarendon, VT 05759-9436 U.S.A.
Tel: 1 (802) 773 8930 | Fax: 1 (802) 773 6993
info@tuttlepublishing.com
www.tuttlepublishing.com

Japan
Tuttle Publishing
Yaekari Building 3rd Floor
5-4-12 Osaki
Shinagawa-ku
Tokyo 141-0032
Tel: (81) 3 5437 0171 | Fax: (81) 3 5437 0755
sales@tuttle.co.jp | www.tuttle.co.jp

Asia Pacific
Berkeley Books Pte. Ltd.
3 Kallang Sector #04-01
Singapore 349278
Tel: (65) 6741 2178 | Fax: (65) 6741 2179
inquiries@periplus.com.sg
www.tuttlepublishing.com

GPSR representative
Matt Parsons
matt.parsons@upi2mbooks.hr
UPI-2M PLUS d.o.o., Medulićeva 20, 10000 Zagreb Croatia

28 27 26 25 10 9 8 7 6 5 4 3 2 1
Printed in China 2508EP